THE MISTLETOE COTTAGES

The Memoirs of a Chartwell Lass

1922-2000

JANE SHERWOOD

ISBN-13: 978-1-723-86462-9

Revised edition November 2018.

Cover illustration also by Jane Sherwood.

Dedicated to my husband Ken.

The Mistletoe Cottages do not and never did exist and neither did Joyce Baxter or her family. Joyce's memoirs reflect the fictional experiences of a naïve country girl with little formal education who lived her whole life in the same tiny cottage that just happened to be part of the Chartwell estate, owned and occupied by Sir Winston Spencer Churchill and his extended family. Joyce's story includes real events and people in the public domain, and great care has been taken to ensure accuracy in their depiction. Any resemblance of the fictional characters to real people, living or dead, is purely coincidental.

CHARACTERS

Joyce Baxter   12/06/1922 - 01/01/2000

Maud Baxter   19/09/1893 - 30/01/1939

Harry Baxter   02/01/1892 - 15/12/1963

CONTENTS

THE MISTLETOE COTTAGES

The Memoirs of a Chartwell Lass 1922-2000

"A Day Away from Chartwell is a Day Wasted."

WSC

My name is Joyce Baxter, I was born on the 12th June 1922 at number 1 Mistletoe Cottages and have always lived in the same house. It is my 75th birthday today and there have been terrible floods all over the country. The little ditch in my garden is now a raging torrent that has broken its banks and the low-lying fields have been transformed into lakes, but my cottage is warm and dry.

I was woken at dawn by squabbling magpies on the roof and have been ironing in my bedroom whilst enjoying a good view of the valley. On returning with a cup of tea there were three adolescent magpies perched on my ironing board, and two on the windowsill. They all flew out the window as I entered the room and joined their parents who were scavenging on the grass below. There is guano all over my ironing board and on the carpet, the birds are cackling and I am not amused. One for sorrow, two for joy, three for a girl, four for a boy, five for silver, six for gold and seven for a secret never to be told.

I have always kept myself to myself and never revealed the secrets of this house to anyone, but before I go to my grave I would like to share what I have seen, heard and been told. It is for you to decide if you believe what I am about to relate, or have I imagined it all?

*****

THE 1920'S.

My parents Maud and Harry Baxter moved in shortly before I was born when my father accepted a job working for Mr Percy Janson at Chartwell Farm. Mr Churchill had just bought Chartwell House at auction from the Colquhoun family, and the Colquhoun's neighbour Mr Janson who lived at Mariners bought the remaining lots including the farmhouse, several cottages and 300 acres of pasture land. He immediately applied for planning permission to build two semi-detached cottages on the old apple orchard down in the valley. The council granted permission only on the condition that these new homes would be made available to working men, and one of those was my father.

The builders discovered a few problems when levelling the ground. This forgotten corner of the farm, shaded by four ancient oak trees on Well Street, had been used as a dumping ground for generations; the ground was sour with all manner of farm rubbish and the ditch carried only a trickle of water down from the Chart Well. Once the ground had been cleared and levelled the traditional Kentish tile hung cottages went up quickly. They were built on a shoe-string, Mr Janson saw no need for foundations, the cottages were not intended to last. Spring water was piped to one indoor cold tap, a copper boiler installed with a tin bath next to the privy and the north facing scullery housed a meat safe. The scullery opened onto the back parlour that was heated by a small solid fuel range. Electricity was not connected, it was considered an unnecessary luxury and not worth the expense.

The Mistletoe Cottages were so called after a very healthy globe of mistletoe that thrived on one of the oak trees. Mr Janson thought nothing of it, but the construction workers were country folk and told each other stories about witches and sorcery deeming the mistletoe oak to be the most sacred of all trees. The Druids believed that the mistletoe seed was sent from the sky in a strike of lightning, and the oak tree was chosen by God himself to protect against witchcraft. The chippy working on the cottage roof was of Viking descent and refused point blank to go near the tree for fear of bad luck, claiming that tampering with a *misteltein* oak could bring sickness or even death to those who did not respect it.

My parents Harry and Maud Baxter knew nothing of these superstitions when they moved in. They had been married for nearly a year and my mother was heavily pregnant with me. Harry was the new maintenance man at Chartwell Farm, his duties included keeping all the farm equipment in good order and driving the Ford Hercules tractor just purchased by Mr Janson, who wanted to increase the efficiency of the farm with less man and horse power. Mr Sykes, the farm bailiff was an experienced ploughman and preferred working with horses. He thought the new tractor a fearsome beast that required the employ of a proper mechanic to operate and maintain all the new-fangled equipment that came with it, and welcomed my father as his assistant.

Mum told me that Dad was an engineer who worked in the print, but after the war when he returned to Waterlow's as a machine minder he couldn't tolerate the print room when all the presses and binders were working to full capacity. The noise took him straight back to the trenches, and one morning he was found cowering in the stock room, shaking from head to foot. The medical officer diagnosed "combat stress" and suggested an alternative outdoor occupation. One of the Waterlow brothers was an old school chum of Mr Janson (Eton I think) and knew he was looking for men to employ on his new farming venture down in Kent. Mr Waterlow had been advised by his overseer that my father was trustworthy and hardworking and put his name forward with excellent references.

Mum's parents were market gardeners in Cambridgeshire. They lived on a smallholding and Mum was the youngest of ten children. Maud met my dad Harry in Wisbech before the war when she was working at Balding & Mansell as a paper folder in the new printing works. She was originally put into service at the age of fourteen, but she didn't like it and ran away. Harry had been sent from Dunstable to train staff on a new printing press. Every day as Harry marched across the factory floor he winked at Maud, and one morning he asked her to afternoon tea at his lodgings, a Quaker working men's club, the St Peter's Institute.

Their courtship flourished until Harry got his call-up papers in 1915 when he signed up with The Royal Cambridgeshire's and was sent straight to The Somme. While Harry was away three of Maud's brothers were killed in action, which sent their mother into a state of great despair. My grandmother threw herself into the river in an attempt to kill herself. She was dragged out alive but died from pneumonia two weeks later despite constant nursing from my mother. Mum was glad to put all that sadness behind her. My parents had a simple wedding with no photographs because they were both in mourning, but looked forward to a better life with their new family in a pretty cottage with running water, an indoor toilet and a garden.

The day I was born Mum said her labour pains started before Dad had gone to work on the Thursday morning, but she didn't want to worry him. Childbirth was women's work and the midwife was calling in on her round that afternoon. By dinner time the pains were coming fast, it was a busy time of year on the farm and Harry had taken a cold pie and some cheese to eat at work. Mum went next door to ask Florrie for help, she had become a good friend, her husband Bert was a stockman and worked with Dad up at the farm. They were older than Mum and Dad but a kind and friendly couple, and Auntie Florrie (as I called her) was always willing to look after me, she was a nice lady.

Florrie didn't have any children of her own but her sister did and she had helped deliver two of her nephews. Auntie Florrie told me years later that the midwife arrived on her bicycle just as my head appeared, and I was delivered there and then by the

15

midwife, much to Florrie's disappointment who said she'd done all the hard work. When Dad came home at six-o-clock for his tea Mum was sitting up at the parlour table with me in her arms, just one hour old and Dad was

"over the moon".

Mum rested a bit, but she hated being idle and two days later she was scrubbing the kitchen floor just to make sure it was properly clean after all the unmentionable goings on involved with childbirth. The smell of carbolic soap was ever present in our house, Mum had a thing about hygiene and if she couldn't scrub things clean she painted them.

Dad's parents were Wesleyan Methodists, they met at Sunday School and attended bible classes throughout their lives. Granddad Baxter died from the Spanish flu shortly after Harry returned home from the war in 1919. There had been a terrible epidemic and thousands of people died all over the country. Nanny Baxter became even more religious after her husband died. She read the bible out loud at meal times and in the evenings long into the night, both before and after she went to bed. Dad was her eldest and stayed for a short while to help her out, but he told Mum when they got married that he was pleased to escape the fire and brimstone. All his brothers and sisters moved abroad to Canada and Australia and left Nanny Baxter at home still reading her bible out loud to an empty house. My parents were happy and content; they had fallen on their feet. They loved each other, had good employment, a smart new cottage and a baby. What more could they want?

Auntie Florrie's husband Bert had worked for Mr Sykes before the war up at Mariners Farm. He was conscripted and then invalided out quite early on because he had been blinded in one eye from a gun accident. He always said he was lucky to be alive, he was in the trenches and his mate had been cleaning a charged gun, the trigger was pulled by mistake and Uncle Bert was hit by the stray bullet.

He was a good stockman and Mr Sykes suggested to Mr Janson that Bert would be the right person to build up the dairy herd on his newly acquired farm. Dad got on well with Mr Sykes and their employer. Mr Janson lived at Mariners throughout the summer months, but his main residence was in London. Dad also liked his job tinkering with the tractor and all Mr Janson's new bits of machinery. He was pretty much left to his own devices and knew little about farming practises, but he quickly learned from Mr Sykes and Uncle Bert.

Uncle Bert loved working with animals. He gave all his cows names, he reared his own hens for eggs, some very noisy cockerels for the pot, and he kept ferrets for rat catching and hunting wild rabbits. When I was little I loved feeding the hens and collecting the eggs with Auntie Florrie. She would give me eggs in exchange for vegetables that Dad had grown in our tiny front garden. Dad spent every daylight hour out there when he was not working, and liked a bit of competition at the village show. He also joined the church choir; he was a good singer. Mum and I both loved listening to him practise, he would sometimes sing me to sleep with a popular tune from the war, or a hymn. My favourite was "All Things Bright and Beautiful". Mum liked the hymns too and we regularly walked to matins on a Sunday morning across the fields and back. She wasn't much taken with the sermons but she said it was worth the walk for the music.

Mum kept herself busy with domestic duties. It wasn't a chore for her, she loved cleaning, cooking and ironing and was very good at knitting and crochet. She wasn't so keen on the washing but she shared that task with Auntie Florrie who made light work of it all. Mum taught me how to crochet but I was never as good as her, she made the finest most beautiful doilies and dressing table sets, and sold some in aid of the church at the fetes and bazaars. She tried to teach me to knit but I am left handed and she gave up. She said it wasn't natural and I should try harder with my right hand.

Dad told me that from the day he and Mum arrived Mr Churchill had got the builders in up at Chartwell House and it was all very disruptive to everyone, especially for the farm. The workers took it all in good heart and were amused at Mr Churchill's ambitious schemes for the house and the gardens. The old gardener Mr Waterhouse had worked for the previous owner and stayed on to look after the gardens when the house was empty, but he struggled to keep things going. Now everything was overgrown and to add to his problems the whole place was a construction site. Dad said he was a nice old chap who was very knowledgeable about vegetables. He always beat Dad at the horticultural show and usually won a few trophies.

Mr Waterhouse had a large family and Dad felt a bit sorry for him. Dad said he had been thrown in at the deep end with Mr Churchill, who took him on because the Reverend Colquhoun said he knew a lot about Chartwell's waterworks! He certainly had the right name for it. Mr Waterhouse tried his best with the help of his son and got roped into all sorts of hair brained ideas that Mr Churchill had, such as levelling lawns, diverting the natural springs, building dams and draining the lake. A couple of years after Mr Churchill took up residence the old gardener decided to retire and went to live in Westerham. I think Mr Churchill helped him find a house and get settled. Dad visited him sometimes if he was on an errand down in the town and they would chat about vegetables and the goings on up at Chartwell.

Mr Waterhouse was still the head gardener when ambitious plans to dam the lake were announced by Mr Churchill. Throughout that summer six extra hired hands were employed in addition to his own staff and he even called on the services of his chauffeur and security man Sergeant Thompson. The project continued for years, long after Mr Waterhouse retired. I grew up with Dad's weekly reports on the progress and many mishaps that occurred each week. Mr Churchill could often be seen working with great gusto along with his children and anyone else who took the slightest interest. The workers at Chartwell Farm enjoyed watching the flurry of activity and sometimes helped out, particularly in later years when the works threatened to swallow up some of Chartwell Farm's pastures. There were lots of disasters. Mr Churchill had a small railway built to carry diggers and move mud from one place to another and was obsessed with the idea of water gardens that became more complicated week on week. I think Mr Churchill could be a bit of a tyrant sometimes, but he was friendly towards the workers. He had great respect for the working man. Dad said he was always the first to greet them with the time of day when he was out and about.

When I was two years old the Churchills had their first family Christmas at Chartwell, but they still weren't there much because the following January Mr Churchill was offered the post of Chancellor of the Exchequer and moved into number 11 Downing Street. He came to Chartwell as often as he could but only for very short visits. Dad was pleased that Mr Churchill and the Conscrvatives were back in power because Mum told me that he thought that would be an end to all the troubles after the war. That same Christmas Mum felt sick all the time.

Apparently she had fallen for another baby. Mum didn't understand then how babies happened, she thought she had to want one in order to get pregnant; Dad wanted a boy but Mum didn't want anything. She worked much too hard keeping the house spick and span along with all her other chores and lost the baby at six months.

I don't remember anything about it but apparently Mum became depressed and struggled to look after me. I was often sent round to Auntie Florrie who was always pleased to see me, but Dad thought his wife should be able to manage. He had recovered from his illness and Maud must pull herself together. Mum lost another baby the following Christmas and was very sad all the time. Harry's strict Wesleyan upbringing made him impatient with his wife and his intolerance made her worry even more. I think she fell for a fourth baby but she lost that very early on; I just remember her crying a lot.

On Friday 30th June 1927, two weeks after my fifth birthday, Mum collapsed in the scullery. I remember the date because the day before Dad had made us all get up an hour earlier than usual to see the moon hide the sun. He had bought a booklet which I still have; "The Daily Telegraph Guide to the Eclipse".

It cost one shilling and explained that the phenomenon (as they called it) must not be viewed with the naked eye. Dad smoked some broken glass in the range the night before in preparation for the viewing, but it was all a bit of a disappointment. The morning was dark and drizzly and nothing much happened. I would much rather have stayed in bed. Mum thought the total eclipse was unlucky. Donkey Jack, a gypsy who lived up on the common, had told her it was a bad omen that would bring disease and pestilence. I was a bit scared.

The following morning it was too wet to go outside and I was playing with Mum's button box in the front parlour when I heard a terrible crash. The last Friday of the month was always small boiled laundry day when Mum put all our soiled underclothing, sanitary towels and handkerchiefs on the range in her stove boiler. She hated this job because all the snot, blood and other unmentionable crusty substances would form a bubbling mess on the top of the pan, and the secret to perfect whites was to carry out at least two skims before adding the soap flakes.

I ran in to find Mum collapsed on the floor. The scalding hot pan was on its side with dirty boiling water spilling all over.

She yelled at me to keep away and go fetch Auntie Florrie. I was crying and did as I was told. I couldn't speak but Auntie Florrie grabbed my hand and we both ran back to find Mum doubled up in pain and crying. Auntie Florrie helped her onto a chair but she was holding her stomach in agony. I was told to stay with Mummy and not go near the washing while she fetched Daddy from the farm. I sat as still as I possibly could and held Mummy's hand; it seemed like forever. Dad was in the stable talking to Mr Sykes and on hearing the news he ran back across the fields so fast that he couldn't speak when he burst through the back door. He whisked me up in his arms and took me into the front parlour and slammed the door shut. I was there all alone and crying.

Meanwhile Florrie went off to the big house where she found Fred the coachman and asked him to get someone to ring for the doctor. The surgery was a long walk across the fields up on the ridge but his wife answered the phone. Fortunately he was at home, and he drove around in his motor car within the half hour. Auntie Florrie had taken me next door to help her pod some peas; I always liked doing that because she let me eat as many as I wanted. The doctor told Dad that Mum's condition was very serious and he took her straight off to the cottage hospital where he carried out an emergency operation. Mum told me later it was a duodenal ulcer that had burst and if the doctor hadn't operated so quickly she would have died from blood poisoning. I didn't see Mum or say goodbye and was not allowed to visit her. Dad told me she was very ill and needed to stay in bed for a long time.

Auntie Florrie looked after me while Dad decided what to do, I even slept next door in a great big bed that she told me was kept for very special guests. Hospital visiting hours were on Wednesday and Saturday afternoons. Dad only went a couple of times because he couldn't get the time off work and no children were allowed in any of the wards. Dad then decided that it was too much to ask Auntie Florrie to look after me for more than a few days and I should go and stay with Aunt Emma, one of Mum's sisters who lived in Wisbech.

Mr Janson had recently returned home to Mariners for the summer and Mr Sykes told him all about my mother and explained that Harry Baxter needed a few days off to go up to Wisbech. Mr Janson was most concerned and offered to drive us to the railway station in his smart new motor car. I had never been in a car or on a train before and it was all very exciting. I sat in the back of the car with the luggage. The leather seats smelled of polish and were very slippery, my feet did not reach the floor. I was surprised how fast we went and it was very bumpy along the lanes down to Brasted.

The train was not at the station when we arrived but we didn't have to wait long. The Westerham Flyer puffed and tooted its way through to Dunton Green where we waited for an even bigger train to go to Charing Cross. We walked through hot noisy tunnels to catch another train that went underground to Liverpool Street. I didn't like it, it was dirty and swarming with people, everything was very loud. Once we left London we were back in fresh air again with miles and miles of fields on the way to Cambridge where we had to change again at Ely before arriving in Wisbech. The further north we went the flatter the countryside became, it was hay making season and the fields seemed to go on forever with a mixture of horses, carts, tractors and hundreds of families working together. Many of the children waved as the train passed and the engine driver hooted in reply with lots of sooty smoke raining down on us through the open windows.

It took all day to get Wisbech. Auntie Florrie gave Dad a nice picnic for the journey with cold rabbit pie and pound cake. He read stories to me and I slept a little bit. When we arrived at Aunt Emma's the street looked really dirty and all the houses had tiny front gardens. Aunt Emma's had a highly polished tiled path leading up to an enormous front door. Dad rang the bell and a very stern looking lady opened it. They shook hands and Dad introduced me to her.

"This is my little Joyce."

Aunt Emma forced a smile and showed us straight up to the box room which was to be my bedroom. Dad put me to bed in a funny old cot that was really low on the floor. He gave me a big hug and told me to be a good girl for Aunt Emma. The room was small and damp with a tiny window and piles of laundry stacked up all over the place, there was barely enough room for the bed and I felt like a sack of old laundry. I fell asleep and Dad left; he lodged the night at the St Peter's Institute and departed the following morning without coming back to say goodbye. I was sad and frightened.

When Mum came out of hospital she needed to convalesce and went to stay with her youngest sister Rose who lived by herself in a place called Waterbeach. Dad could not afford to take any more time off so Uncle Bert took Mum and Auntie Florrie in his tumble cart to catch the train at Brasted Station and they met Auntie Rose in Cambridge where Auntie Florrie left them and returned home. Waterbeach was not very far from Wisbech but I don't think anyone gave me much thought, they assumed Aunt Emma was taking care of me and that I was in the best place, but I knew I wasn't. I was scared of Aunt Emma. The house was dreary with a small back yard and no flowers. Wisbech was a horrid place and Aunt Emma was horrid as well. She was a war widow and took in laundry to make ends meet. Looking back, I think she struggled to manage but she never told anyone, she pretended everything was fine. I think she took it all out on me, she was a miserable woman with no patience and her teenage sons were not very nice to me either.

I was used to having lots of cakes and sweeties when I was little, I think it was Mum's way of showing she loved me and consequently have always been a bit plump. I also have a stigmatism and have had to wear glasses from a very young age. My cousins teased me relentlessly calling me fatty four eyes and they did their best to make me cry so that I would be threatened with the pantry where Aunt Emma told me the snakes would get me if I made a noise. I was terrified. I had nothing to do for a whole month. Aunt Emma made me play in my room and the only time we went out was Sunday chapel. That was very different to church. There were other children there but Aunt Emma didn't mingle with the congregation, we marched straight back home afterwards. I quietly cried myself to sleep every night until one Sunday after chapel Aunt Emma announced that I was to start school the next morning. She left me with a very stern schoolmaster who sat me at a high wooden desk at the front of the class. I didn't know anyone and no-one talked to me, they said I talked funny. I really missed Mum and Auntie Florrie, I hated Dad for leaving me in such a horrible place and thought I was never going back home.

At the end of November on a cold damp Saturday morning Aunt Emma woke me very early and told me to pack my suitcase because we were going to visit her sister Rose. Mum often talked of Auntie Rose, her favourite sister, so this was very good news. We went to the same railway station that Dad and I had arrived at in Wisbech and that made me even more homesick. We were only on the train for a little while when

Aunt Emma started bustling about and when the train stopped at Waterbeach she bundled me out of the carriage like a sack of washing.

It was just a short walk from the railway station to Aunt Rose's tiny little cottage that was squeezed between a baker's shop and a tumble down double fronted house with giant steps that rose up above my head. Aunt Emma knocked on the cottage door and who should open it but my Mum, she gave me a huge hug and we both cried with happiness. Auntie Rose was waiting inside the tiny dark room which looked a bit scary but I didn't care, I was back with my Mum and Auntie Rose looked nice. They said I could stay with them both until Mummy was well enough to travel back to our house. Aunt Emma could not wait to get away. After a quick cup of tea and a rock cake she rushed off to catch her train. I had so many questions: Were we going home? Did I have to go back to that horrid school? Would I have to see my cousins again?

We all slept in the back room at Auntie Rose's. She didn't have an upstairs even though it looked like a house from the outside. The baker lived on the floor above, over his shop and Auntie Rose's house. Every morning at 3 am he started work kneading the bread and loading the ovens. It made a terrible clatter and kept me awake, but Auntie Rose and Mum slept through it all. Auntie Rose was a shop assistant in the bakery and worked from seven-o-clock until dinner time every day except Sunday, and always came back with a nice treat for our tea.

The plan was for us all to go back to Chartwell the following Sunday when Mummy would be well enough to travel and Auntie Rose could come with us. We all walked to Waterbeach Station and Mum bought the tickets for the three of us to London. Then that funny old underground train and finally Charing Cross to Dunton Green where Dad met us off the train in Uncle Bert's tumble cart, because it was cheaper than catching The Westerham Flyer to Brasted. Mum and Dad were so pleased to see each other that we all cried and then Dad hugged me. I was so happy. Mum was very, very thin and the journey really tired her but she soon perked up with a nice cup of tea and some of Auntie Florrie's scones with butter from the farm and her delicious strawberry jam. She had also made up her spare bed that was only for very special guests like me and Auntie Rose.

Mum was much improved, Auntie Rose stayed for a whole week and we were all very sad when she went back to Waterbeach. She said if she stayed any longer she wouldn't have a job or a house to go to. Auntie Florrie and Auntie Rose got on like a house on fire and after Rose left Florrie fussed over us all like a mother hen. I was very, very, happy. Mum and Dad said I didn't have to start my new school until January and we had a lovely Christmas together with lots of singing at the church, and there was a party up at the farm. I was very shy and remember thinking that I must stay with Mummy all the time to stop her getting ill and going away again.

The night before I started school I cried all night and felt sick. Mum tried to make me eat something but my tummy was upside down. I cried all the way to school across the wet fields and Mum was crying too by the time she left me with my new schoolmistress, Miss Prett. She had a purple nose but a kind face and smiled as she took my hand and led me off to my desk that I was to share with Millie Dopson who had already been at school for a whole term and was very nice to me. She liked to make me laugh and very quickly we became best friends, but she lived just a few yards from the school and when I came home there was no one to play with. I didn't mind because I had Mum who was well again and she along with Auntie Florrie taught me all sorts of things that a girl should know such as baking, laundry and needlework.

Everything was back to normal at home and then Mr Janson died. His son wasn't interested in keeping things going and the farm was sold to Major Pilbrow who owned a large estate in the next parish. He was a retired soldier who had served as an officer in India where he also owned a very swish hotel. Dad said Mr Sykes respected him as a good gentleman farmer who knew what he was doing because he always got lots of rosettes in the local and the county shows.

Major Pilbrow had a stern manner, as many military men do, but Dad said there was nothing wrong with that. There was a lot of coming and going between the Major and Mr Churchill who was still carrying out extensive landscaping, and they joined forces on a few projects. Between them they arranged for a long drive to be constructed down to Chartwell Farm from the main road, which eased access to the working barns and cottages behind. Mr Churchill also wanted to move the footpath that ran through his garden. Major Pilbrow objected to start with, but Mr Churchill was a persuasive man and the

Major gave in eventually along with the Parish Council who had chipped in with lots of objections of their own. There was another footpath that ran down the edge of the woods and across the fields. Uncle Bert was annoyed about it, he said

"the footpaths were being used by blasted gongoozlers who did not abide by the country code and they were disturbing his livestock.
All they were interested in was trying to get a glimpse of Mr Churchill and
wandering about where they had no right to do so."

*****

THE 1930'S.

Dad got on really well with Mr Churchill's chauffeur Howes, Dad called him Sam and said he was a very clever chap. Major Pilbrow agreed to let Mr Churchill rent one of the farm cottages for Sam while his own chauffeur's cottage was being rebuilt, and Dad got to know him really well. They were always talking shop (as Dad called it) about mechanical matters and he respected Sam as a highly skilled driver and engineer. Both of them had learned to drive during the war but neither of them had a driving licence as it had only just become compulsory.

Apparently, Mr Churchill once got a warning letter from the Metropolitan Police claiming that Mr Howes was not licensed to drive and therefore driving illegally without insurance. Sam thought the whole episode a great joke and delighted in telling Dad all about it. He married one of Mrs Churchill's parlour maids, they moved away after a couple of years and eventually went to America where he became an extremely successful businessman. Dad missed him a lot and they lost touch because neither of them were very good at letter writing. Mum and Dad were invited to their wedding but they didn't go because I had just come home from hospital after recovering from scarlet fever. Half the school went down with it one day, the headmaster lined us all up in assembly and told us two ambulances were coming to take us all off to the cottage hospital where we were put in an isolation ward.

I was terrified and cried the whole time, I didn't want to leave Mum again. Millie tried to cheer me up but I was inconsolable, we didn't get any visitors and I thought I was going to be in there for the rest of my life. The nurses were very strict and everyone was frightened of Matron. The only good thing was the chocolate biscuits, we were allowed one every afternoon with a glass of milk. Mum came to collect me after about three weeks and we walked home together. That felt like the longest walk I had ever done in my life, but it was only a couple of miles. Mum put me to bed and bathed me with calamine lotion three times a day, it was nice when it went on but then it dried hard and smelled funny. She also cooked me special things like egg custard, milk jellies and a lot of stewed apples, but the best thing of all, I was allowed to eat as many boiled barley sugars as I wanted.

Jack Smith was a gypsy known to all the locals as Donkey Jack. He often passed by the cottage and always stopped to chat if anyone was about. He never failed to mention the mistletoe in the oak tree saying it was a very rare beast and should never be tampered with. He and his wife Mary earned their living by gathering fruit, flowers and greenery from the hedgerows and both knew a lot about ancient remedies passed down through their Romany families for generations. Mr Sykes said the gypsies did far too much scrumping for his liking, but Dad said they were harmless and only harvested what no-one else wanted. Donkey Jack gave Dad some ointment made from foxgloves for me, but Mum wouldn't use it because she said she didn't know where it had been.

Donkey Jack died soon after that and Mr Churchill arranged his funeral because Mrs Donkey Jack didn't know how and had no money. A few of the locals attended, including Dad and Uncle Bert. The following Christmas Mrs Donkey Jack asked the gypsies from the lower common if one of the young lads could help her gather mistletoe to sell in the town. The youngster passed our mistletoe oak on his way to Mary's shack and scrambled high into the branches to pick a fine clump for the old lady. She was rather alarmed when he told her where it came from but she would get a good price and in her eyes the damage was already done. In the spring she received an eviction notice from the council because someone had complained that her shack was built illegally and needed planning permission.

Mr Churchill was rather cross about it all and said she could camp in his woods with her two dogs. She managed for a while until she was knocked down by a workman on a bicycle and broke her ankle. Mr Churchill also said that she could drink from his water tap in the stable yard, but now it was too far for her to walk and she started drinking from Major Pilbrow's stream.

I was about twelve and remember it really well; Mr Churchill had already upset lots of the locals because he had filled his new swimming pool with water from the mains without permission and all his neighbours' taps had run dry. There had been a serious drought for months, even during the winter and there was talk of water rationing, people in London were having to queue for water with their own buckets. The water company told Mr Churchill to only fill his pool at night, but he was impatient and told his men to fill it nonstop both day and night. It didn't affect us at home because we were on piped spring water but it meant Major Pilbrow had no water for the farmhouse and he was furious.

He also complained to Mr Churchill about the old lady who was stealing water from the spring that fed our cottages. Mr Churchill thought the Major was being very mean to Mrs Donkey Jack who meant no harm, but Major Pilbrow was adamant that she was breaking the law. The arguments went back and forth for several months, but eventually the matter resolved itself when Mrs Donkey Jack died from some sort of influenza. The locals said it was Weil's disease caused by drinking infected water, but we drank the same water and we were fine.

I looked forward to school now that I had made friends and liked my teachers. I was an eager scholar, I enjoyed learning poetry to recite and Dad would help me practice. I was also quite good at sums and top of the class in mental arithmetic when we had to stand at the front and recite our times tables. My favourite subject was needlework. Mum taught me how to crochet and I used to help Auntie Florrie cut out papers for her patchwork quilts. Our teacher, Miss Prett, taught all the girls dressmaking and I loved it.

I am left handed which probably meant I got a little bit more attention than the others and I think she liked me, she always asked me in preference to the other girls to make her camiknickers because she said I could sew the smallest neatest hem stitches. I was very pleased to sew for my teacher and it boosted my confidence no end. At home I liked making my own little rag dolls and dressing them in all sorts of fancy outfits with tiny felt shoes, hats and little miniature handbags. I helped Mum with her darning and repairs and she said I was very neat but she didn't really approve of my dollies, she said I made them too frivolous.

Mr Sykes had a wireless up at the farm and when Mr Churchill was broadcasting a speech, all the men would gather round to listen. Dad often brought home Mr Sykes's old newspapers and read them avidly even when they were a week out of date. He worried about all the bad news in Europe and the speech that Mr Churchill made the week after Armistice Day in 1932 really got him agitated, he was convinced there was going to be another war and often repeated Mr Churchill's words.

"We are no longer safe in our island home."

This didn't help Mum with her nerves and there was a bit of an atmosphere in the house. Dad was on a very short fuse and took his anger out on the vegetable patch, every single clod of earth was double dug to a fine tilth. Looking back now I think this was when Mum's illness started although she hid it very well. Her father, Granddad Wargent had been poorly for a while but she never went to see him. Aunt Emma was looking after him in Wisbech and Mum didn't want to visit for all sorts of reasons that she said she didn't want to talk about. I certainly didn't want to see Aunt Emma or my horrible cousins. The sisters exchanged letters and Auntie Rose kept Mum informed but after Granddad died Mum refused to go to the funeral even though we were all invited. Auntie Rose went and wrote to Mum afterwards telling her who was there and how things went. It made Mum very sad and she said she just wanted to forget it ever happened.

Up at Chartwell when Mr Waterhouse retired the new head gardener moved in straight away to the old gardener's cottage with his wife and two daughters, Doris and Gwen. Mr Hill had been under gardener at Breccles Hall where friends of Mrs

Churchill lived. He was an experienced flower gardener who also knew a lot about the management of lawns. Mr Churchill agreed that he should have more staff to enable the garden to become more productive in flowers, fruit and vegetables. What Mr Hill didn't know was that he would very quickly be introduced to landscaping on a massive scale with Mr Churchill's grand plans for extensive water gardens. It seemed like every time Mr Churchill finished one lake, he wanted to excavate another, only to discover problems of monumental proportions; he dug ponds and lakes and even two swimming pools that all failed in some way and usually leaked. His latest plan was to turn the lake peninsula into an island which proved to be an extremely expensive and hazardous exercise that took years to complete along with many arguments, not only with his contractors, but also with Major Pilbrow.

Dad said there was always an issue of some kind or another cropping up between the two landowners. They had meetings about drainage, cess pits and the water supply, but Mr Churchill was very adept at getting his own way. Major Pilbrow enjoyed making minor criticisms of Mr Churchill's farming activities, such as telling him his apple trees needed pruning or his hay was not good enough for the Major's dairy herd. The hay issue was thoroughly supported by Uncle Bert who only wanted the best feed for his beloved animals, he treated them like they were his own children. However, when the Major agreed to let a cottage to Mr Churchill for his chauffeur Howes, the two men became more amenable.

Mr Churchill's newest landscaping plans required the dumping of several tons of earth, sludge and gravel that were to be dug out of the lake. It was agreed that both the farmyard and a large hole behind the cowsheds could be used for this purpose. Major Pilbrow had just built a new cowshed and the ground needed to be levelled. He had also employed a new bailiff who was to arrive when the cowsheds were ready for use, which Uncle Bert was rather worried about; he didn't like change.

The building of the island in the lake provided both amusement and concern to everyone on the estate. The lake had to be drained before work commenced, which proved to be a very tricky undertaking. Mr Churchill had found a local contractor who was willing to rent him an excavator which led to a whole series of problems including the wrong size tracks, bad weather and mechanical failings. Work started in January but everything took many times longer than expected and the digger was not up to the job. The weather had been terrible, it rained almost constantly since the start of the project and now it was March and "the animal" (Mr Churchill's nickname for it) after breaking down several times had sunk deep into the mud at the bottom of the lake. Four hydraulic jacks had to be brought in to lift it out along with railway sleepers to support it, but as they and it sank deeper and deeper, it took nearly a week to rescue the machine. They then had to lay sleepers all the way to the gate to stop it sinking again whilst being transported. The huge task was eventually completed largely due to Mr Churchill's obstinacy, as he so famously said;

"Never, never, never, give in."

I don't know what Mr Hill thought of all the goings on but he carried on doing his routine jobs, one of which was spreading nitrate of ammonia on the lawns in the spring. In April the children's nannie goats were let out to graze near the house and were both poisoned. Sarah and Mary were very upset, particularly as the goats had been named after them. Nannie goat Sarah died, but Mary was given castor oil and survived along with her kids. The same year some of Uncle Bert's cows lost their calves and milk production was down, he mentioned to Dad that he thought the ground could be contaminated but that Major Pilbrow had dismissed the idea. All the cow slurry used to wash down from the top fields and settle in the valley near our cottages to drain into the stream. Dad said the manure was good for his vegetables but the smell could be terrible on a hot day after it had rained and in the winter the lane was impassable.

In 1935 King George celebrated his Silver Jubilee and Dad bought Mum a very special souvenir book illustrating twenty-five years of the king's reign in photographs from 1910 to 1935. Mum and Dad looked at it a lot and talked about the events featured in it. I liked looking at all the funny old clothes everyone wore, especially before the war. Dad told me that Mr Churchill was First Lord of the Admiralty during the Great War but for some strange reason he wasn't mentioned in the souvenir book once. Dad said the conclusion at the end summed up everything that was good about England.

"In these quiet green pastures "under an English heaven"
is the everlasting symbol of that peace and beauty which
all mankind desires. Even the silence here speaks of a great
content, of faith in simple things. And set beyond the tree

fringed hillock is the horizon of Hope – hope that the years
to come may be rich and fertile, free and peaceful in the
green fields of the motherland that gave us birth."

I left school when I was 14 and was offered a place at the
secretarial college in Croydon, but Dad wouldn't let me go
because it was too far away. I could have gone by Green Line
bus from Westerham, but he was adamant that I should stay at
home and he would find me a job up at the farm. Thinking
back, I wonder if perhaps Dad could not afford the fees or the
bus fares, but he never said anything. I started doing a bit of
cleaning and liked helping out in the milking parlour; it also
gave me a chance to visit Mr Churchill's pigs, the baby piglets
were adorable little creatures.

I only worked mornings, Dad and I would walk up to the farm
together at first light and most days we both walked home
again across the fields at dinner time for one of Mum's
delicious hot meals, before Dad went back to work in the
afternoon. When there wasn't much meat for the table she
would make Yorkshire puddings with lots of gravy. I still like
that as a meal nowadays with freshly dug vegetables from the
garden. In the afternoons I helped Mum, she often did some

baking after her morning chores were done and could make a small amount go a long way. I loved her rice tarts made with semolina and home-made raspberry jam.

We were very lucky and rarely went hungry, Dad got free milk as part of his wages and Uncle Bert was a good shot despite only having one eye. On Sundays after milking when we went to church with Auntie Florrie, Bert would take his ferrets and his shotgun out with the gamekeeper who lodged up the road, and he usually came back with rabbit, pigeon or pheasant. Sometimes he gave us squirrel which Mum made into pie but I didn't like that. Bert's chickens were always trying to get at Dad's vegetable patch, they would often fly over the fence and peck at their favourite currants and berries. Dad said Bert should clip their wings but Uncle Bert didn't want to do that because then they had no escape from the foxes. Dad set up all sorts of contraptions with net, string and tin cans to stop them and Mr Churchill's pheasants, not to mention the wild birds damaging his crop. He didn't complain too much though because Uncle Bert was always very generous with his game.

That same year, Nanny Baxter came to stay for a week, she was still reading her bible aloud and kept me awake at night until the early hours reading the Old and the New Testament. She was a stern lady and ordered Mum about, telling her she was doing everything the wrong way, but she was quite kind to me. She told me all about her travels across the Atlantic in a huge ship to visit her daughters in Montreal, and how she wished she could go and live there too. Dad asked if she had heard from his brothers but she said not. Uncle Eric was in the army and Uncle George went to Australia after Dad had a row with him because he got a girl in the family way and didn't want to marry her. I wasn't supposed to know that, but Mum told me one day when I started bleeding down below and she was explaining about periods and babies and how to make sanitary towels that had to be strong enough to be boiled so they could be used over and over again.

Nanny Baxter brought me a present "The Mammoth Wonder Book" an illustrated collection of poems and stories by famous people like Charles Dickens, Hans Anderson, Longfellow and Sir Walter Scott. I loved all the poetry and read lots of the stories but one stood out; a scary tale called "Baldur", the Norse god of light who dreamed that he was going to die. He was the son of Odin and Frigga and when he told Frigga his dream she made everything in the world swear not to harm

Baldur, but she forgot the mistletoe plant because it was so small. An evil spirit called Loki wanted Baldur dead and persuaded Baldur's twin brother Hodur who was blind to throw a mistletoe dart at Baldur and it killed him. Odin then had another son called Vali who killed Hodur by a single blow when he was only a day old.

"He then spent the rest of his life trying to lift the shadow of death from the face of the weeping earth."

The story reminded me of the twenty-third psalm that I learned off by heart at school. I worried about the valley of the shadow of death, even though it said I would fear no evil. Nanny Baxter explained that as long as I said my prayers every night the good Lord would protect me. Mum and Dad didn't pray every night; did that mean they were going to die? I told Dad about the story and he said I was being silly.

That was the only time I ever met my grandmother. When she left she kissed us goodbye and Dad took her to Westerham in Major Pilbrow's new van to catch the Green Line bus to Victoria and make her way home to Dunstable on the train. She gave Dad quite a lot of money, I think she knew she wouldn't see us again. Dad bought me a new bicycle and Mum a nice comfy velvet lounge suite with a settee that folded down into a chaise longue which Dad insisted on calling "a put you up". Mum thought it all very extravagant when there were lots of other things we needed, but Dad just laughed and said he had put plenty in his National Savings at the post office for a rainy day.

The following winter King George died which was all very sad so soon after the silver jubilee celebrations. His son Edward was heir to the throne but there was no coronation because he abdicated soon afterwards. Dad always said he was feckless and didn't deserve to be king; he certainly wasn't as popular as his father. I clearly remember the day of his abdication speech. Dad heard it at work and came home really angry.

"What was the King thinking of,
not facing up to his responsibilities?"

Mum was upset too but I couldn't see what all the fuss was about. The King wanted to marry an American divorcee but the Church of England said it was against the rules so he chose his true love over his kingdom. I thought it all very romantic and was a bit jealous of Mrs Simpson. I wished I had a prince to rescue me from my boring life, but I didn't tell anyone. I think Mr Churchill felt the same because he stuck up for Edward which made him very unpopular in the Houses of Parliament. Eventually it was all sorted out and Edward's brother George became king instead and the coronation went ahead as planned in May 1937. George was already married with two daughters and people said he didn't really want to be king, but he did his duty and in Dad's eyes that was all that mattered.

Now that Mr Churchill was not in the cabinet he was able to stay at Chartwell more often, and he was writing another book - or I should say a series? "The History of the English Speaking Peoples". One of his secretaries, Miss Hamblin told Dad that the great man often worked long into the night and expected his staff to be available for dictation at all hours. Miss Hamblin grew up in the village and knew all the locals, her parents lived along the ridge on a neighbouring farm and she was well liked. Anyone wanting a bit of gossip would get short shrift from Miss Hamblin, she kept a lot of things under her hat but not all the servants were as discreet and sometimes Dad would come home with talk of high jinks in the household, or news of a famous visitor. Everyone always knew when Mr Churchill was under pressure because he resorted to staying in Orchard Cottage instead of the big house where he liked to write uninterrupted.

Once the whole family had moved in properly to Chartwell House they opened their gardens to the public, initially in aid of the Kent Nursing Association. That caused a bit of grumbling down on the farm because the traffic blocked the lane every time there was an open day. The following year they detailed an AA man for parking duty and there was even more traffic. I was given a collection box and told to stand down by the exit as people departed in their fancy cars. I enjoyed doing that and seeing all the beautifully dressed ladies and gentlemen who came to visit the gardens in the hope of a glimpse of Mr Churchill. They were unlucky though, he always made sure he was otherwise engaged on the open days and was usually up in London. There were rumours that Charlie Chaplin came to visit, but I never saw him. I did like watching his films though. Millie and I used to cycle down to Westerham sometimes to watch a matinee at The Swan Picture Hall that showed lots of good films; I liked Fred Astaire too.

Mum started losing weight again and lost her appetite. Dad made her go to the doctor who said that she might benefit from radium treatment, but there was nowhere local and Mum didn't want to travel. She carried on as best she could but she was getting weaker every day and Dad said I should leave the farm and stay at home to look after her. One day the air raid warden, who we knew from church, came around on his bicycle to issue us with gas masks. Mum got really panicky and refused to try hers on. He suggested using me as a guinea pig. It was horrible, he tightened the straps too much so I couldn't breath and the rubber smelled dirty. Mum's gas mask never got worn, it was put under the bed and that's where it stayed. After just a few weeks she was unable to stand and had to be helped to the wooden commode that stood in the corner of the room. The doctor called around more often and injected her with morphine which made her sick and gave her hallucinations. One night she thought soldiers were trampling all over the garden and coming in to shoot all of us; it was just the old mistletoe oak blowing in the wind.

I was kept very busy at home with all the housework and the cooking but when my chores were done I would sit with Mum and read to her. Dad sang to her in the evenings when he came in from the garden. Towards the end she wanted the paraffin lamp constantly burning low day and night and wanted me to sit with her all the time. She was terrified of dying alone in the dark and would frequently call out for Dad to comfort her in the middle of the night. On Christmas Day, Dad and I sang carols around her sick bed and I read letters from Auntie Rose out loud. She slowly deteriorated over the next month and died on the 30th January in 1939 when I was sixteen. She had a horrible death and literally wasted away with so much pain but at least she died at home with Dad and me at her bedside. I still miss her.

Dad grieved quietly and became obsessed with the troubles in Europe, listening to all the news whilst at work and reading all the newspapers he could get his hands on. He explained to me all about the Spanish Civil War but I wasn't really interested. In March, Hitler invaded Prague and Dad was beside himself with anxiety; in April Mussolini invaded Albania and Dad became even more distressed. Throughout this time there was a lot of coming and going up at the big house and Mr Pilbrow had absented himself from Chartwell Farm, it was rumoured he had gone abroad. On the 1st September it was announced on the wireless that Hitler had invaded Poland. Two days later we were up at the church tidying after matins when the churchwarden's wife came running in to say that the Prime Minister, Mr Neville Chamberlain, had announced on the wireless that Great Britain was at war with Germany.

Everyone gasped and quietly made their way back to their homes. It was a long walk for us across the fields and we walked in silence. As soon as we got home Dad burst into tears and hugged me so tight I couldn't breathe, he sobbed and sobbed and so did I for what seemed like forever. Then Dad gathered himself and took the roast breast of lamb out of the range while I cooked the vegetables that had been prepared before church. He ceremoniously carved the meat just the same as he always did and I served up new potatoes, runner beans, carrots and thick Bisto gravy. There was an apple and blackberry pie for pudding. I asked Dad if he wanted me to make some custard, but neither of us was hungry and the pie got left on the side until tea time. We never mentioned the crying ever again but I think we were closer.

The next day it was announced that Mr Churchill was once again First Lord of the Admiralty which seemed to please Dad, he said he was back in his rightful place. The Churchills all moved away and Chartwell House was given over to two families who were evacuated from the East End, but they only stayed a couple of weeks, they didn't like living in the country and went back to London. The house was dust sheeted and closed up. There was another very large house up on the hill that had stood empty for years and one day there was a terrible commotion with lots of crashing and banging echoing around the valley; the house was being demolished. Mr Sykes said that the people who owned it couldn't afford to repair it, which seemed a terrible shame but the gamekeeper told Uncle Bert that Mr Churchill had ordered the house to be knocked down because it was too dominant a landmark and he wanted to confuse the Luftwaffe. That put the wind up me a bit, but then I thought at last something might happen around here!

Dad started paying into the Rural Pennies Scheme. Everyone up at the farm contributed, it was to raise money for the Red Cross and they wanted volunteers to help with fund raising. I helped a bit down at the church and the churchwarden suggested that Millie and I should do a first aid course. The classes were held in a big house along the ridge. I used to cycle up there before the others to help make the sandwiches. The lady of the house always praised me for my bread cutting skills, I could get more rounds out of a loaf than anyone else and she said my Mum had taught me well. I was also very proud to finish the Red Cross courses and get two certificates, one in "First Aid to the Injured" and another in "Home Nursing". I received a thank you letter from the Duchess of Marlborough for all the money I collected in aid of the Red Cross Agriculture Fund.

Everyone was issued with leaflets ordering us to put crosses of sticky tape on all our windows to prevent them from shattering if a bomb was dropped on us. Dad was insistent that we do it immediately and it threw me into a bit of a panic. He went off on his bike to Wright's in the village to buy brown paper tape, but they had sold out and he had to cycle to the town to see Miss Evenden in the hardware shop. She always had plenty of everything and Dad benefitted as a regular customer from her reserve store of No 8 batteries that were kept under the counter. We put a cross on every single window pane in the cottage on the inside which made them impossible to clean and blocked most of the light.

Then we were told about blackout curtains, the thick black cotton was 4/6d a yard in the haberdashers. We couldn't afford to make curtains for all the windows so Dad cardboarded the bedroom windows and I made folding blinds on the downstairs windows. I managed to make them all from just three yards of material and Dad told Mr Sykes how clever I was. Mr Sykes asked if I would make blackout blinds for him and he paid me a few shillings for doing so. That really boosted my confidence. The cottage was now really dark and dreary and we had to have a lamp burning in the parlour all the time, it reminded me of Mum.

*****

THE 1940'S.

Mr Chamberlain was forced to resign in 1940 and Mr Churchill became Prime Minister and Minister of Defence just before the Battle of Britain began. The Churchills didn't live at Chartwell at all during the war, it was considered too dangerous for them to stay there, but not for us! In the summer of 1940 troops from the 7th Corps of the Canadian army led by Brigadier Hertzberg moved into the woods behind Chartwell. It was their job to camouflage the lake; they drove hundreds of stakes into the mud and covered the water with brushwood to alter the aerial landscape. They also syphoned off the middle lake and disguised the swimming pool. Poor Mr Hill the head gardener was going spare, all his hard work was being undone and the troops created a terrible muddy mess.

The bombing started soon after that. German planes would pass overhead every night, you could almost set the clock by them, they usually appeared just after seven. Sometimes enemy planes flew over during the day and dog fights were a regular sight, the Battle of Britain was taking place literally above our heads. In addition to the bombers we could also see search lights high up in the sky beyond the hill towards London and hear the Ack-Ack guns in the distance, it was all very eerie and rather frightening. When the German planes were driven back by the guns they dumped their bombs any old where and one very bad night several bombs fell in the space of about two hours on and around the estate. One huge crater was found the next morning in the top field and it took every man available several days to clear up the debris, including Dad and Uncle Bert who was extremely worried for his cows.

Our cottage didn't have an air raid shelter, we could have run up to the farm and sheltered in the cellar but Dad thought it was too dangerous to run across the fields, so when the sirens went off we settled ourselves in the parlour with a pack of cards and a Monopoly board that always had a game in progress. My game piece was the thimble and Dad the top hat. Dad insisted on being the banker but I did beat him sometimes with all my properties. We were lucky, the bombers always seemed to miss Mistletoe Cottages, maybe because we were hidden by the trees. Perhaps our mistletoe oak was protecting us. We were also told by the air raid warden to collect our ration books from the post office and were issued with stamps for fuel, bacon, butter, and sugar.

Dad struggled a bit to get enough fuel up at the farm, but we managed quite well for food, we often got a little extra butter and cream from Bert which no one knew about. I did miss not having enough sugar for my baking though and tried all sorts of recipes from the newspapers. Dad really liked "Brown Betty" a pudding made from stale breadcrumbs, apples and golden syrup. People said that the queues for rations were terrible in London but they weren't too bad in our little village. I always cycled to the shop and enjoyed chatting in the queue. Millie was usually there and I often went around to her house afterwards for a cup of tea before cycling home again.

On the 8th March in 1941 Nanny Baxter died and Dad was given a week off to make the funeral arrangements. We went up to Dunstable by bus and train to sort out the house. The journey was a bit tricky because Dad had never travelled from Westerham to Dunstable before, and all the road signs and names of stations had been taken down to confuse the Germans! Well, it certainly confused us. Dad's sisters couldn't travel from Canada and Dad tried to contact Uncle Eric with no luck. He didn't even bother to try and find Uncle George, I don't think he ever knew when his mother had died. Lots of people from the chapel came to the funeral and one very kind lady called Ethel, who said she was a close friend of Nanny Baxter, put on a simple spread for the wake in the meeting hall. They were all a bit fire and brimstone and Dad didn't like it.

The house was very neat and tidy with a few nice pieces of furniture. Dad gave everything to the Wesleyan Chapel, apart from an ebony clock, lots of sheet music and a piano which was delivered to our cottage a few weeks later by two men who had attended the funeral. Petrol was rationed, but one of the men had a delivery van assigned to war work, and he was able to divert to our house from Dunstable on his way to Dover whilst collecting some munitions for the Home Guard. The piano was installed in our parlour, it was beautiful; figured walnut with pearl inlay and brass candle sconces. Dad started playing straight away and it seemed to cheer him up. I learned how to play a few tunes and we had sing-songs in the evenings. Dad no longer sang in the choir, he had stopped going to church because he didn't like the new vicar; he said he was a Lefty, but it was nice to hear singing in the house again.

There was some gossip in the town that Mr Churchill might be coming back to Chartwell, but nothing came of it. Later in the year Major Pilbrow wrote to Mr Sykes to tell him he was selling the farm and that Major Marnham would be moving into the farmhouse. Uncle Bert, Dad and the other workers were called to a meeting with the new Major who explained he was keen to expand the livestock and that Mr Churchill had offered him some extra grazing which would involve more work. There was also talk of Land Girls coming down to help. None of the men were very keen on that idea but I thought it would be nice to have some girls to talk to. Mr Hill wasn't very happy either, he had been told to plough up his beautiful lawns and was not too keen on digging for victory after all the upheaval with the Canadian Army. He said he had enough to do with the large kitchen garden, especially now he had lost two men to conscription.

In April Canadian troops returned to Chartwell. This time it was men from the 1st Division, they requisitioned some pasture and occupied the woods, where they dug trenches and erected barbed wire fences. At night there was a constant rumble of army vehicles manoeuvring in the woods and the lanes were filled with military traffic both day and night. The bombing was still going on and some people in the village said the Canadians were putting us all at risk because they were noisy and not always in total blackout. Every couple of months the regiments were changed and hundreds of new soldiers led by a band marched up Well Street from I don't know where, past our cottages and up to the woods where they were billeted in tents. We could hear the band from miles away, they were very good and everyone came out of their cottages to wave and cheer as they marched by in their smart uniforms; they looked so handsome.

I sometimes went for a walk in the woods near the camp and one day a couple of squaddies asked me if I had a friend and would I like to go dancing in the town. I told Dad about it and he said he wanted to meet these boys first and that I should invite them round for Sunday tea along with Millie. I made egg sandwiches and rock cakes and Millie brought a cucumber from her Mum's greenhouse and some beetroot. The boys arrived in their uniforms with nylons, chocolate and cigarettes. Dad accepted the cigarettes gracefully but was very quiet. I think he still bore a grudge over losing his sister to a Canadian when she eloped back in 1914, especially when his other sister followed her to Canada and neither of them ever came back.

That's when I began smoking, Dad always smoked roll-ups but I liked the smart Canadian cigarettes. Millie and I started going to dances with the Canadian lads, there was a dance on every Saturday night somewhere or other. They would pick us up in a jeep and always had something with them to boost our rations, like a bucket of dripping or a sack of sugar. I made myself two new dresses out of some old curtains I had bought at a jumble sale and Millie asked me to make her one too. Word soon got around and I was being asked to make loads of things. I told people that I could make anything if they could get hold of the material. I even made a wedding dress for a girl from the village out of a parachute someone had found in the fields down by the river.

I also discovered a love of dancing; Glen Miller was all the rage and the Canadians knew all the latest dances. The jitterbug was the best, and there was one lad called Hank who was a very good dancer. I really liked him, he was a bit older than me and had a mass of black curly hair with lovely hazel eyes. I was no lightweight but he could swing me under his arm, over his shoulder and through his legs with no trouble at all, and after we won first prize at a dancing competition we started dating. Dad was a bit frosty to start with but Hank had a nice way with him and they chatted about tractors and engines. Hank was from Vancouver Island and his father was killed in The Great War; now he wanted to do his bit and Dad respected that.

We dated for a few weeks and then Hank's regiment was moved to Surrey, he did get some time off and came to stay but never more than a few days. Hank also had a good singing voice and Dad liked playing old music hall tunes with us all singing along; not quite Glen Miller but good enough. On the 20th May 1943 Hank presented me with a solitaire opal ring and asked me to marry him. We got engaged with Dad's blessing on the condition that we would not marry until the war was over.

It was my twenty-first birthday on the 12th June and Dad bought me a second-hand treadle sewing machine. The lady who owned the haberdashery shop down in the town had mentioned to Dad that she was replacing hers with a modern electric machine and knew I did a lot of sewing. It meant I could work faster and be more professional. I used the spare bedroom as my sewing room with a view across the fields beyond the mistletoe oak. The windows captured the afternoon sunshine and in high summer there was not a better place to be, I was in love and happy.

Shortly after that Hank was sent to Aldershot and at the end of March in 1944 he wrote to tell me that he, with thousands of others, was waiting to go across to France. He was given seven days leave in May and came to stay for a few days. We had been engaged for a whole year and had a lovely time together. We went to the flicks, had picnics down by the river and danced our last jitterbug in the town before he went back. I didn't hear from him again. I often chatted to Millie while we were queueing for rations in the village and she told me that the other lads thought Hank was married with a wife in Canada, but I couldn't believe that. Anyway, I never heard from him again and don't know if he lived or died.

A few weeks later I thought I might be having a baby; my periods had stopped and I felt sick all the time. I was frightened to tell Dad, but he noticed I wasn't well and thought I might be getting an ulcer, the same as Mum. I was losing weight and one day something happened, I was suddenly bleeding quite badly from below and I think I lost a baby. Fortunately I was at home alone and never told anyone. Dad knew I was sad and told me not to fret about Hank, neither of them ever knew about the baby and I think Dad was secretly pleased that Hank had gone.

It turned out that all the training in the woods and everywhere else had been in preparation for Mr Churchill's secret plan for D-Day on the 6th June 1944, and what a well-kept secret it was. On that same day Chartwell had its own little tragedy. Mr Hill the gardener had been into hospital for a minor operation when they discovered he had leukaemia; he died on D-Day leaving a wife and three children. Mr Churchill had been concerned that his beloved Chartwell might be targeted by the Germans and the Hill family had been told to move into the servants' quarter to protect the house. It was all very unsettling for everyone and the bombing raids were relentless.

When Mr Hill died it fell upon Mrs Hill to run the garden as best she could until Mrs Churchill could find a replacement head gardener. We all tried to help out a bit but it was a real struggle for her, and one day she was working in the kitchen garden with her two youngest when a German fighter plane flew down low and fired a battery of bullets all along the wall. They weren't injured, but it was a shock to all of us.

Many of the local houses had been damaged by incendiary bombs but it was still thought to be safer than living in London. A few yards from Chartwell on the other side of the road there is a long thin building called Little Mariners that used to belong to Mr Janson. At the time it was being used for evacuees, and there were over twenty children, mothers, babies and eight nurses staying there when the roof was hit by an incendiary bomb. They were told it was too dangerous to stay in the house so everyone was moved to a bigger house up on the common where it was thought they would be safe. Three weeks after D-Day a doodlebug hit that house and killed all the occupants outright; it was so very sad that those poor children had been brought to a place of safety on two separate occasions only to perish.

Mrs Hill took it badly so soon after her husband's death and was very relieved when Mr Harris the new gardener arrived, only to discover that he and his wife were to have her beloved cottage, and she was expected to move into a smaller house on the estate. Dad and I were pleased that our cottage wasn't part of Mr Churchill's estate and that Dad's job was safe up at the farm. Major Marnham was a good employer and a conscientious farmer who paid considerable attention to improving the pastures, repairing fencing and building up the dairy herd, and he appreciated his staff.

The doodlebugs and the V2 bombs were terrifying. One of them exploded in mid-air over Chartwell one night and covered the fields and gardens with jagged metal. Mr Harris had been provided with a gang of Italian and German POWs to help with the clearing up. They were put under the supervision of Sergeant Major Whitbread, who was retired from the army and had worked for Mr Churchill for many years. Major Marnham also had German prisoners clearing up all the mess the Canadians had left behind in the woods, and now they provided much needed manual labour.

Dad knew the Sergeant Major well and called him Tiggy, they used to have friendly arguments about politics. Dad said he was a bit of a Lefty and a hard task master but a very fair man. The POWs were used to hard work and after they had cleared away all the barbed wire, de-camouflaged the lakes and cleaned up the swimming pool they were put to work on the farm. When they were not needed by Major Marnham they were requisitioned by Mrs Churchill to clear footpaths and repair walls, and in return they were offered billets on the estate.

Dad befriended one young lad called Albert who had joined the Hitler Youth when he was only sixteen years old. The Germans sent him straight to the front with almost no training where he was captured immediately by the allies. He was then marched to a POW camp in Belgium where he stayed for a few months before being shipped with hundreds of other prisoners to England and put to work on the land. He was originally billeted at a German hostel up the hill and had to report back by sundown every day to his overseer, Herr Schubert.

The men were accustomed to taking a short cut through the woods to Chartwell, but when they were discovered doing so Mr Churchill complained to Herr Schubert that his men had been trespassing. This triggered a little bit of ill feeling. Albert was from the Black Forest and said no-one ever stopped him walking in the woods back home. He did however walk the long way around from then on and was very pleased to accept a billet with several other men in a cottage on the estate. He chose not to return to his fatherland after the war, his village was near the Austrian border and under Russian occupation, the wrong side of The Iron Curtain.

May 1945 was an eventful month for everyone. On May Day the newspapers reported that Hitler had committed suicide and the Germans surrendered in Italy. The following Friday we were told the Germans had surrendered in Denmark and by Monday an announcement was expected from the Prime Minister. We went up to the farm to listen to the six-o-clock news but it came and went without comment, so I came home and left Dad up there. Then about half past seven Mr Churchill came on the radio and announced that tomorrow, Tuesday the 8th May, would be the first VE day, Victory in Europe. Dad didn't arrive home until after eight-o-clock but he was very excited. Mr Sykes had tapped a barrel of beer and everyone was celebrating, we were all very happy indeed. Many speeches followed and I too went up to the farm to listen to the radio as much as I could.

On the 23rd Mr Churchill was reinstated as Prime Minister when the coalition government resigned and a general election was called for the 5th July. The war really was over. There were reports of everyone going mad in the cities and towns all over the country, but here everything carried on as normal, the cows had to be milked, the pigs fed and the hay cut but there was a huge sense of relief and Dad was the happiest he had been since Mum was alive. The Churchills came back to Chartwell on the 18th May and Mr Churchill stopped on route to make a speech in the town to huge crowds. We walked up to the house along the main road to welcome Mr and Mrs Churchill back home with a few of the locals. We had to wait ages. It was well past teatime when they arrived, but such a very happy day.

The Churchills moved back to Chartwell in October 1946, although they seemed to be away on holiday most of the time. On the 15th October Chartwell Farm was sold and we discovered that Mr Churchill was now our landlord and Dad's employer. I don't know where he found the money to buy the farm but he obviously thought he could afford it. It was all a bit of a surprise because people had been gossiping in the town that Chartwell House was for sale again and that Mr Churchill had lost all his money, but everything carried on as usual. We discovered much later that some of Mr Churchill's friends had bought Chartwell House for him and offered it to the nation on the condition that Mr and Mrs Churchill could live there for as long as they wanted. It didn't make any difference to us at the time although after that when they opened the gardens to the public the traffic was terrible, so many people wanted to see where Mr Churchill lived.

It turned out that Major Marnham had been approached by the chief agricultural officer for Kent. Mr Cox was keen to expand the county's dairy industry by finding more land in the area suitable for that purpose. He was a very knowledgeable gentleman and advised Mr Churchill that Chartwell Farm would be a good investment with a view to increasing production. Uncle Bert didn't want to work for a new boss, he said he was too long in the tooth to start with new ideas. He had been suffering from bad headaches and was nearing retirement age and Auntie Florrie wanted to move down to New Romney near her nephews and nieces. I was very upset. Auntie Florrie had been like a mother to me and Dad would miss Bert dreadfully. Mr Sykes also decided to retire leaving just Dad, who had no choice but to stay on.

A new dairyman moved into number 2 with his wife and two children, they were pleasant enough but we both missed Bert and Florrie. They didn't stay long, Reg and his wife complained at the lack of electricity and that the bathing arrangements in the cottages were not up to scratch even though we had managed for twenty-five years ladling hot water from the copper to the bath with only oil lamps and a range for light and heating. Mr Churchill told his agent to get rid of the family because he said Reg was very stupid. I think he probably was, I remember one evening just as the light was fading I could hear someone hammering in the lane. The noise echoed all around the cottages and I went outside to find Reg banging a nail into the mistletoe oak. He doffed his cap and said,

"Good Evening Miss Baxter, I's just nailing this tree to get rid of my toothache, it's giving me terrible gyp."

Number 2 stood empty for a few weeks and then the Browns moved in, and how we wished they hadn't. Mrs Brown was a lazy woman and heavy with child. They already had eight children who ran riot all over the fields and up in the woods. There were always children crying, fighting or throwing stones and they all swore like troopers. At night there would be screaming and shouting, especially after Stan and Betty had been on the beer. Sometimes they came to blows. Stan was a small brawny man with a bad temper but capable of very hard graft, a very useful farm hand along with his two eldest sons who worked with him. There were five boys and three girls all crammed into the tiny cottage, and they had no respect for it.

When Betty had her fourth baby girl she sent one of the boys up the oak to collect some mistletoe for the cradle. I saw the mistletoe in the pram and was worried that the berries might poison the poor little mite, but Betty said it was to stop her being snatched by the fairies. I didn't say anything but thought to myself those would be very brave fairies to venture into the Brown's house. Soon after that they were moved up to a bigger cottage over the hill where their eldest daughter had a baby boy when she was only fourteen. Betty brought him up as her own, but he didn't thrive and grew up a bit simple; I wondered if Betty thought the fairies had anything to do with that!

Shortly after Christmas we heard that Mr Churchill had purchased even more land beyond the woods and up the hill, including several cottages and another farmhouse. Mary, Mr Churchill's youngest daughter, married Captain Christopher Soames in February and they moved into Chartwell Farmhouse once it had been done up a bit. Captain Soames was put in charge of all the Chartwell Farms, and the first thing he did was to check all the workers' cottages and arrange for the cottages with no electricity to be connected. I was so excited I didn't mind the mess, we were given a ceiling light with a switch in every room and an electric socket in the parlour.

There was a double switch on the staircase so we could turn the light on and off at both ends, no more trailing up the stairs like Wee Willy Winky with oil lamps and candles. The scullery was fitted with a cooker point and they gave me a brand new electric cooker with a special reserve battery to kick in for when the power dropped on a Sunday dinner time when everyone was cooking. It took me a few days to get used to it, I kept forgetting to turn it on. The first thing Dad did was buy a radio and we sat and listened to it together in the evenings while I did my sewing.

Dad bought me "The Book of Good Housekeeping" for Christmas because he said it had a very good chapter on soft furnishings that could help me with my sewing business. Dad had inherited a love of books from his father who worked as a proof reader at Waterlow's until his premature death at the age of forty-nine. I found the book fascinating, especially the chapters on colour schemes and home decorating. I set about painting the whole cottage in lovely light bright colours and made some new curtains. I even emptied out the coal hole and white-washed it before the coke was delivered for the range that we still had in the parlour.

There was a lot of information about things I thought would never concern me, such as "The Problem of Domestic Help" and "Entertaining". I couldn't see me ever having a general maid or arranging a formal dinner party, but I read the book from cover to cover and learned a lot of new things. As it turned out that knowledge came in quite useful later on when I was still working up at the farm.

Next door was still empty and Mrs Churchill had arranged for it to be smartened up a bit so that some Land Girls could move in. They were a cheerful bunch and a few years younger than me, but Dad said they were wild and I shouldn't fraternise with them. Most of them were Londoners who loved a party. Different girls came and went, they all had bicycles and used to ride around in the dark to the local dances and the flicks. Dad said it was too dangerous and wouldn't let me out at night on my bike even though we were no longer in blackout. Sometimes there would be ructions if one of them tried to sneak a man in late at night. Dad did not approve at all and did not like them working on the farm, he said they didn't know what they were doing and made twice as much work, but most of them were good sorts and it was nice to hear a bit of laughter.

Captain Soames and Mr Churchill had ambitious plans for the farm; the workers were all a bit sceptical but respected their enthusiasm. Mr Churchill had been sent an enormous Massey-Harris binding machine from Canada and Dad had to get his head round the workings of it. It was the only one in the country and too big really for Chartwell's small rolling pastures, but it was given to Mr Churchill by the manufacturers as a thank you for what he did during the war. Mr Churchill also joined the Shorthorn Breeders' Club and several of the magnificent beasts arrived on the farm to boost the dairy herd. Then some Belties arrived from General Sir Ian Hamilton; they were black and white beef cattle that he had reared himself. One had been born on Mr Churchill's birthday and it was called Winnie. Uncle Bert would have loved that. There were now horses, sheep and even more pigs which were put out in the old orchard behind Mistletoe Cottages, but they made a terrible mess and Captain Soames very quickly moved them up the hill where the ground was dryer.

That same year Mr Churchill was in Marrakech for Christmas, but his wife Clementine stayed with their daughter Mary and Captain Soames at Chartwell Farm for the holiday. Mary was heavily pregnant with her first child due in February and they all had dreadful colds, but Mrs Churchill had arranged a Christmas party up at the big house for all the estate workers' children and their mothers the day after Boxing Day. I went along to help out with the refreshments. It took me out of myself and stopped me thinking about Mum, which I always did at Christmas. It was lovely to hear all the children laughing and watch their faces in amazement at the conjurer that Mrs Churchill had booked for the party.

Mr Harris, the head gardener, died in 1947; I think all the upheaval and extra work had been too much for him, he was never as good as Mr Hill. The new man was called Mr Vincent who moved in with his wife Gwen to the gardener's cottage a few months later. He was a lovely man with a very happy face, and an excellent gardener with extensive knowledge of all things horticultural. His soft Norfolk accent seemed very fitting in his role as head gardener and he was well liked by everyone. He was very kind to Dad's friend Albert, the young POW who was very eager to learn, and Mr Vincent was a patient teacher.

Mrs Churchill attended the Chelsea Flower Show that year and saw a gold medal winning rock garden which she immediately purchased for Chartwell. The design had to be considerably enlarged and adapted to fit the chosen space by the spring just north of the house, and it was made up of Welsh sandstone that had to be shipped in on huge lorries. Mr Jones the designer supplied his own workforce, but Mr Churchill insisted that his workers should help, and that included Albert. The project continued for months and was very impressive when finished; a huge rocky outcrop with water cascading down and stepping stones across the goldfish pond to a lovely old Japanese Maple. Albert was very proud of his part in that project, and he later used what he had learned to develop his own ideas with stone walls and water features. The pond became a favourite spot for Mr Churchill. He would sit in the sunshine and feed his golden orfe or sometimes paint there, always with a cigar and usually a strong drink.

Captain Soames boasted an impressive army career but was invalided out after the war shortly before he married Mary Churchill. He was one of the hunting, shooting and fishing crowd who were all very posh, but he knew a bit more about farming than Mr Churchill. He was a good manager and had a hands-on approach when supervising the various different farming activities. At hay cutting time he could be seen out in the field shooting rabbits as they fled the thresher; sometimes

Mr Churchill joined him. Mrs Soames had also served in the army during the war and the household was run with military precision. I helped out in the farmhouse sometimes with a bit of cleaning and also some mending, sewing on buttons, things like that.

Mrs Soames had her first son on the 22nd February in 1948 and the christening of Arthur Nicholas Winston Soames was held at Saint Mary's Church in Westerham. The event attracted a lot of publicity with film crew and reporters everywhere, it all seemed like a lot of fuss and bother to me. The baby was always called Arthur when he was little, I can't remember when people started calling him Nick. They very quickly had a little girl after that called Emma and it was lovely to see the children playing in the gardens on the farm and up at the house. Mr Churchill was very good with children and an excellent grandfather.

Now that The National Trust owned Chartwell they wanted to open the gardens to the public just for a day a few times a year, beginning in the summer of 1948. The first opening brought scores of cars that blocked Well Street and the main road; it seemed like thousands of people wanted to see where Mr

Churchill lived or maybe even meet him, but he made sure he was never there. Some days the traffic jams were almost back to Westerham and Dad got very grumpy because the lane down to the farm got completely blocked, making it really difficult to get the tractors out for haymaking. It was much worse than when Mr Churchill opened the gardens for charity before the war, but it was still only a few days a year.

*****

THE 1950'S.

Mr Churchill was Leader of the Opposition in January 1950 and had to cut short his holiday in Madeira because the Labour Party was forcing an early election on his party. Captain Soames was also running as a Conservative candidate for Bedford despite being ill with a duodenal ulcer. They both fought the election and saved their seats, but Labour won by a majority of five votes. The result being that both men had less time to devote to the Chartwell farms leaving everything quietly ticking over at home while they spent much of their time canvassing and on political business. One morning there were a few reports in the newspapers that Mr Churchill had died the night before. This shocked Dad and me, but it turned out to be a malicious rumour. Miss Hamblin told Dad that Mr Churchill thought the reports hilarious and quickly gave a statement saying that he

"knew the rumour suggesting that he was dead to be untrue".

The Soames children had a nanny and sometimes when I was working in the farmhouse they would be watching a programme called "Watch with Mother" on their television.

Emma was too little to understand but Arthur liked Andy Pandy, a puppet dressed in striped pyjamas who lived in a laundry basket with Teddy and Looby Loo, a rag doll. Nanny told me that Miss Lingstrom, a lady who lived in a cottage up on Well Street with her friend Miss Bird, produced the programmes in her shed. Between the two of them they made the puppets, wrote the stories, the music, narrated it and presented it all themselves on the BBC.

I was delighted, I knew the ladies by sight. We always passed the time of day when out and about, I had no idea how clever they both were. I met Miss Bird on the farm footpath a few days later and told her how lovely I thought their children's programme was. She was a very quiet, reserved person, but she thanked me and said she would pass on my kind words to Miss Lingstrom. They always smiled whenever I saw them after that.

The following year Mr Churchill became Prime Minister again in the autumn, but throughout the summer he stayed at Chartwell as much as possible and was racing to finish the fifth volume of his epic "History of the English Speaking Peoples". If I was on an errand up in the north field I usually walked through the water garden and often saw Mr Churchill sitting on his garden chair feeding his fish. He always acknowledged me, and one morning he called me over and told me to stand very still. A robin was hopping about near the pool, Mr Churchill held out some food and the little bird came closer and took it out of his hand. It was so lovely to see and Mr Churchill chuckled with delight. I thought I might try that at home although I didn't have much time to sit about waiting for little birds. Soon after that the Churchills were back in Downing Street, although I don't think either of them were in particularly good health and their daughter was pregnant again with her third child; there was a lot to do down at the farmhouse.

Two weeks after the anniversary of Mum's death King George died, he had been ill for a while but why do these things always happen near Christmas? His daughter Princess Elizabeth was married with two young children and the family were on a tour of the Commonwealth. She was called back to England immediately on the news of her father's death, and because she had no brothers she was heir to the throne. I felt quite sorry for her, she was four years younger than me with a young family and not only did she have to get over the death of her father, but now she had the responsibility of the whole British Empire on her shoulders. I know she has a lot of support and great wealth but her life is not her own. The rich and famous lead such complicated lives at such speed, I wouldn't want it for all the money in the world.

That same year the vicar from our parish church left under a bit of a cloud. The national press got hold of the story and named him "The Red Vicar". There was a lot of fuss and bother with our local MP who it seems the vicar had insulted and Mr Churchill stepped in and raised the issue at question time in Parliament. When the new vicar arrived with his wife, they discovered that they didn't have much of a congregation. Both he and his wife tried very hard to coax the parishioners back with all sorts clubs and activities, but Dad refused point blank to go anywhere near and said he wanted nothing to do with church or chapel. I would have gone along to a few things and attended on a Sunday sometimes, but I thought it best to leave it. I didn't want to upset Dad particularly at that moment in time because he had heard rumours that part of the Chartwell estate was being sold and he was worried about his job. The rumours came to nothing again though.

Everyone was looking forward to the Queen's Coronation, a bit of good news for a change. Lots of people were buying televisions on the "never, never" especially for the great day because they were far too expensive to buy outright. All the farm staff were told by the new bailiff that everyone was invited to watch the whole event up at the farmhouse because the Soames family were all staying up in London with their children to attend some of the celebrations. Mr Churchill was not only Prime Minister now, but also had been awarded the Knight of the Garter. The Right Honourable Sir Winston Spencer Churchill was an honoured guest in the royal procession along with his wife. Sir Winston looked magnificent in his uniform as Lord Warden of the Cinque Ports and Lady Churchill wore a beautiful silk satin robe with a tiara.

It drizzled all day, but I don't think anyone noticed or if they did, they didn't mind, the pageantry surpassed all grumbles about the English weather. The state coach was a sight to behold in solid gold, it looked just like the fairytale coach from Cinderella driven by eight horses with footmen on both sides. Princess Elizabeth and her husband Prince Philip left Buckingham Palace and travelled down The Mall to Westminster Abbey under beautiful decorations in the shape of crowns. The whole route was lined with servicemen and women holding back huge cheering crowds, the like of which had never been seen in living memory. The procession seemed to go on forever with dozens of coaches, carriages, horses and every possible military rank and uniform one could imagine.

The service was glorious and went on for a very long time, I hoped it wouldn't be too much for the Churchills. The heralds blowing their trumpets were dressed like characters from Alice in Wonderland and the sound was unmistakeably regal, just like in a film I had seen at The Swan Picture Hall about Henry VIII. The Queen's dress was silk and covered with the most beautiful embroidery, her velvet and ermine train carried by six maids in waiting who were followed by the Mistress of the Robes, the Dowager Duchess of Devonshire. How fabulous must it have been to be in charge of that wardrobe and be able to handle all those luxurious fabrics! It was all too much to take in, the pomp and ceremony was something I could never have imagined: the chair of state, the throne, the bishops, and eventually the Queen put on her royal crown, it looked extremely heavy. Immediately a cry of

"God Save The Queen"

rose from the congregation and all the peers and princes, peeresses and princesses put on their coronets to a fanfare of trumpets and a gun salute at the Tower of London.

The television camera showed the Queen's mother in the royal box with Prince Charles, who they said was fascinated with the spectacle, but I thought the little chap looked rather bored. He was standing next to his aunt, Princess Margaret who also looked rather grumpy, but maybe she was a bit jealous? The journey back to Buckingham Palace was even more impressive than the outward journey with the crowds all going mad. Eventually Queen Elizabeth II came out on the balcony with her family to watch a fly past by the Royal Air Force, and waved to her subjects. That reminded me of the war and I think at that very moment the whole country was united in feeling that better times were on their way.

It is well documented that Mr Churchill had a great deal of respect for the Queen, and said that she could not have been more perfect for the role as monarch. Her Royal Highness often invited the Churchills to accompany her entourage in the royal box at the races. The Churchills always accepted, not only because it was a great honour but also Sir Winston genuinely liked the Queen and enjoyed her company and the excitement of the races, even when he could barely stand through failing health. Sir Winston, as everyone now called him, was not very well at all, but he still insisted on carrying out all his engagements particularly while his deputy, Mr Anthony Eden, was very ill himself and unable to work. Mr Eden was also Home Secretary and his absence created double the work for Sir Winston.

The great man had always been a gambler and liked a flutter on the horses; he owned a few that were stabled at Epsom, as did Captain Soames and Sir Winston's horse Colonist II was proving to be quite successful. Urged on by his son-in-law they decided to buy a small stud farm at Newchapel that was roughly half way between Epsom and Chartwell. This new venture distracted them further from the running of the farm; they were beginning to lose interest. In addition to all that Sir Winston was also awarded the Nobel Prize for Literature which required him to make a few personal appearances at various literary events that involved more travels abroad. It was all amazing to me, how one man could be so good at so many things.

Mrs Soames told me that when her son Arthur went to prep school someone told him that his grandfather was the greatest man in the world. One morning in the summer holidays that followed Arthur found his way up to his grandfather's bedroom at Chartwell where he was in bed working, and asked him if it was true that he was the greatest man in the world? Sir Winston was in the middle of dictating to his secretary. He stopped in full flow, looked down at Arthur and said

"Yes, I am. Now bugger off."

In 1954 myxomatosis was running rife throughout the countryside and almost all the rabbits were infected. It is such a horrible disease, the poor bunnies would sit in the fields and along the roadside just staring into space with big red weeping, vacant eyes. It was a blessing when the foxes took them or even when they got run over, anything to give them a speedy demise. Captain Soames said that the foxes were killing all the game birds, his poultry and some of his piglets because there were no rabbits left. I am not sure if that was true, there were still plenty of rats, mice and voles running riot in the hay meadows and large flocks of wild birds nesting in the fields and hedgerows. I think Sir Winston and Captain Soames were particularly worried because they had just bought a Swedish Landrace boar along with a family of sows and piglets at huge expense, and they didn't want the foxes to eat their investment.

Captain Soames still loved his hunting and as a member of the West Kent Hunt, he would ride with them each winter season galloping across the fields and up and down the lanes with a pack of hounds in hot pursuit of the wicked foxes. I have always thought the whole idea of fox hunting rather silly. Foxes are clever and more often than not able to outwit all the smartly dressed gentlemen and ladies in their red and black coats with their magnificent horses, hunting horns and baying dogs making a terrible kerfuffle and getting in the way of honest folk trying to carry out their daily duties.

I was also very surprised to discover that a gentleman who lives in the next parish and owns a vast amount of land both locally and further afield, has ancestors who adored fox hunting so much that they introduced foxes to the Isle of Wight in order to practice fox hunting as a sport whilst they were holidaying at their island estate. I do wonder if gentlemen and their love of sport always have the best of intentions when it comes to preserving wildlife and the countryside, particularly when you see how some of them behave.

Sir Winston did not go out with the hunt any more, he was not very well at all and I think many people (including his family) thought he should resign as Prime Minister, but he was obstinate as usual and carried on regardless. Lady Churchill had been abroad recuperating from her own health problems, and Mrs Soames had yet another baby; they now had two boys and two girls. Eventually the date for Sir Winston's resignation was made for the 5th April 1955 and it was announced on the radio that evening.

He spent the following day debriefing at number ten and after a little cocktail party arrived back at Chartwell in the evening to get away from the press and the public. A holiday to Cyprus had been arranged and they departed two days later, but they were not gone long because it rained the whole time and they came back early. Captain and Mrs Soames made sure they were suitably entertained and rallied round with lots of visitors to keep them amused for the next couple of weeks, which kept all the staff very busy and I was called in for extra duties.

Dad found Mr Cox to be a knowledgeable and conscientious farm manager and all the work was dealt with very efficiently. I think the farms had run at a loss for many years and Mr Cox said he had never expected to stay long, he knew he had only been employed to cover while Sir Winston and Captain Soames were too busy to manage the estate themselves. Mr Cox took it upon himself to take responsibility for rerouting many of the ditches and replanting the hedgerows with the help of half a dozen labourers, including Dad's friend Albert. This was a good lesson for Albert, he learned a lot about water courses and the way natural streams behaved and that influenced his future projects. The improved drainage helped the pastures a great deal, particularly down in our neck of the woods.

Dad and I always thought that the Soames family would stay forever because Mrs Soames loved Chartwell so much and had grown up there, but it was not to be. Captain Soames bought a country house near Tunbridge Wells and the family moved down there with their four children. Sir Winston put Chartwell Farms in the hands of the estate agents Knight, Frank & Rutley, many of the animals were sold off and the property auction went ahead on the 18th June 1957. Mr Cox stayed on to manage the remaining livestock at Chartwell House, which Dad was pleased about, although he was a bit worried that the new owners may not want his services, or mine for that matter.

The farms and the estate including our cottages were sold to Mr Christopher Mann, who had several businesses including a share in Mayfair Films. His wife was a famous Australian concert pianist called Eileen Joyce. Mr and Mrs Mann both travelled a lot, they owned a flat in London and had recently sold a dairy farm in Oxfordshire that boasted a substantial herd of Jersey cattle. Albert was now married to a girl from the next parish, and the new owners gave him the job of under gardener for the farmhouse gardens which came with a new cottage that Captain Soames had built further up the lane.

I was anxious that we might have to move but Mr & Mrs Mann assured Dad that his job was safe as their general maintenance man, despite him being of pensionable age, and they still wanted me to help in the house. Our new landlords were good employers and Dad was left to get on with his work without much interference. They also brought with them a new farm manager called Mr Denning who moved into the farmhouse up the hill. He was an amiable chap and got on well with everyone. My anxiety proved to be unfounded.

Eileen Joyce practiced her piano for six hours every day despite suffering from rheumatism. Her beautiful music room faced the midday sun with a magnificent view across the sloping pastures to the woodland. The same view that Sir Winston had fallen in love with thirty years earlier. Both Dad and I loved listening to her practice when the windows were wide open in the summer and music wafted across the meadows on the prevailing wind. I liked working for Mrs Mann, she was a very glamorous lady and quite beautiful with piercing green eyes. I loved cleaning her boudoir and looking after all her fabulous dresses, many of which were designed by Norman Hartnell.

She told me that when she was performing she wore a different coloured dress for each composer; Bach was black, Beethoven blue, Tchaikovsky red and for some reason that I never really understood, Debussy deserved sequins! She did have a bit of an artistic temperament but Mr Mann was a very calm man and always smoothed the waters, they were both always very kind to me. Mrs Mann had a son from a previous marriage but no-one ever saw him, he was grown up and lived in Oxford.

Mr Mann was a shrewd businessman and liked to get things done. It seemed they had only been moved in for five minutes when he began negotiations with the Sutton and East Surrey Water Company who wanted to build a reservoir just above the woods and lay pipework to feed the houses in the next parish beyond the valley. The work commenced immediately and much of Mr Cox's and Albert's work was undone with the drainage ditches that had been dug to take the water off the fields blocked and many trees felled. The water company sank pipes in the woods and the old orchard and created a huge quagmire that took nearly two years to dry out. The reservoir rose like a huge pimple on the top field and the comings and goings were endless. Dad said it was like the Chartwell lakes all over again.

The lane was impassable throughout but we didn't complain because in return for all the disruption our cottages were going to be connected to mains water. Our cottage was the first supply off the new pipeline and every year in the spring a man from SESW came to check our water for purity. Dad always thought this unnecessary, after all we had been drinking spring water for the last thirty years with no side effects. I was quietly pleased, I had always wondered about our water, Mrs Donkey Jack, Mum's illness and my miscarriage, but it was all best not mentioned.

Number 2 had been empty for ages, it was only used now to house casual labourers during harvest time and sometimes hop pickers for the neighbouring farms. They could be a rowdy bunch and were not particularly friendly. I really missed Auntie Florrie and Uncle Bert. Lady Churchill had called our cottages little more than slums that were unfit for human habitation and Mr Mann decided to decorate number 2 and make a few improvements. Once it was done he suggested we move next door while they decorated our cottage.

I was very excited although I didn't like living next door, there was a strange chill in the front parlour. We were only in there for a couple of weeks while the electrics were updated and a bright white enamel solid fuel Rayburn was installed in our kitchen parlour to replace the old black range. The oven also fed a new hot water tank giving us unlimited hot water for an upstairs bathroom with a built-in bath, a wash basin and most luxurious of all, a toilet. It meant me losing my sewing room but I didn't mind, it most definitely was worth it. The painters whitewashed all the walls and I set about painting some of the furniture and making new curtains. When we moved back in I felt like I was living in a palace.

Now that we had a selection of electric sockets Dad bought me an electric twin tub with a hand wringer on the top to replace the old copper which we put out in the yard. I still used it with a dolly for boiling up the linens to get them nice and white. I also liked dyeing material that I had bought at jumble sales to make cushions and patchwork quilts, and the copper was perfect for that. Dad let me set up my sewing machine in the parlour with the piano and the "put you up". We didn't use that room very often, the kitchen parlour was much cosier by the Rayburn and that is where we watched our newly acquired television that Dad bought outright from Radio Rentals. I was getting a lot of dressmaking and repair work now from the locals, but it was not regular and I liked working up at the farm. There was always something interesting going on. Mrs Mann travelled a great deal with concert tours in Europe, America and Australia and she needed reliable staff back home at Chartwell Farm to keep everything ticking over.

When Mr & Mrs Mann lived in Oxfordshire they were well known for their Shiplake herd of Jersey cows that were now 100 strong and included many prize-winning champions. Mrs Mann loved the buzz of the showing ring and Mr Denning was very knowledgeable, but he discouraged her from entering shows that were too far afield now they were down in Kent, because it got in the way of his milk production. Mrs Mann loved her cows like pets along with her pigs, hens and two poodles called Crochet and Quaver. I thought it was very funny when she ordered a kangaroo from Harrods to remind her of Australia. Dad was not amused when he was told to help Albert erect a kangaroo proof fence to stop the silly creature escaping and frightening the livestock. I think the poor thing was lonely because it died after a couple of years.

One day, an Australian journalist turned up to interview Mrs Mann who was looking particularly glamourous in a beautiful silk day dress. They took pictures of her cuddling Venus, her prize Jersey cow and then she was asked to feed the chickens and the piglets for a photo shoot. It was all rather silly, she said she liked driving the tractor but she left the milking to her staff. Dad said she'd driven the tractor once and got it stuck in a ditch and she never fed the pigs in a silk dress. Mrs Mann showed me the article when it was printed, she had told them that she delighted at the extensive servants' quarters of her new home

> "as she needed a big staff
> particularly in the cooking department."

She certainly did, they ate very well and did a lot of entertaining. I was brought in for extra duties when there was a social gathering and my Good Housekeeping Book that Dad had bought me all those years earlier came in very useful indeed. I did a lot of swotting up.

A few years later Mr Mann decided the estate no longer needed all the cottages and wanted to sell some of them off. He asked Dad if he wanted first refusal as a sitting tenant to buy our cottage on the understanding that he would still work up at the farm for the same money but shorter hours. Dad was not sure if he should take the plunge, none of our family had ever owned their own house and the purchase would take almost all his savings.

Our friend Albert was offered the same option on his cottage and he convinced Dad that it was a good investment not to be turned down. Albert even took out a small mortgage to buy his cottage, he desperately wanted to own a little bit of England. Dad was nervous but agreed that it would give me a bit of security if anything happened to him. He was getting his pension and his wages on top were a bonus that meant he could still pay some money into his savings each week for a rainy day.

*****

Dad was given responsibility for everything mechanical on the whole estate, including the garden tools and checking that all the motor cars were in good working order. He became a regular customer down at the hardware shop in Westerham and would have long chats with Mr Goose who could patch, repair, and sharpen practically anything that was presented to him. Dad would usually cycle down on his bike, but the farm also had a delivery van for bigger items and sometimes I went with him. I got to know Miss Fleet quite well; she was a bit younger than me and had started as a trainee at Evenden's when she left school at fifteen.

It was not long before we were on first-name terms and Margaret was always very interested in what I was making. I popped into the haberdashery shop every time I was in the town and more often than not I was given a few needlework jobs they had been saving up for me. Everyone was rather shocked when the Beeching cuts were announced and the Westerham branch line was to be closed down. The shop keepers were worried that they would lose business and we all wondered if more buses would be laid on to replace the trains on the already congested roads through the villages from Sevenoaks to Oxted. On some days the traffic would be nose to tail in both directions all the way through the Market Square in Westerham, and further down the High Street where the road is really narrow, and I don't think it was much better in Brasted.

The cottage next door was empty again and Mr Mann wanted to apply to the council to have the agricultural tenancy lifted. He suggested to Dad that if he was willing to share the fees, both cottages could be included in the application. Dad worried about it a lot, but eventually agreed to have money deducted from his wages each week until the debt was paid for and the application went ahead. Once permission was granted everything changed.

In 1961 number 2 was sold to a travelling salesman and his wife for nearly £3,000. Dad couldn't believe it, he had only paid a few hundred for our cottage and now ours might be worth almost as much. The couple who bought number 2, Peter and Olive, were nice enough but Dad said they had more money than sense and I think he was probably right. They were from South East London, newly married and looking forward to starting a family. However, they were never blessed with the patter of tiny feet, which was probably for the best because Peter was away on business a great deal. Olive did not go out to work and threw herself into renovating the house and garden. The building and decorating commenced on a major scale, it was like a small version of Chartwell with something always going on. Work was being done inside and out but their garden still looked like a builder's yard.

What Dad didn't realise when he bought the cottage was that also meant taking on responsibility for the cesspit which was in our garden but shared by both cottages. It was expensive to have it emptied and the house deeds stated that the cost should be shared by both properties. The landlord up at the pub told Dad to put a dead animal in it and let the maggots eat all the shit. Dad chatted up the gamekeeper who brought down a dead roe deer that had been injured in the woods and he chucked it in the manhole. This approach worked well for a while but eventually the pit filled up and the smell was intolerable, it had to be emptied. Our neighbours were happy to pay their share, money was no object to them but it was a big chunk out of Dad's wages, so he managed to eke out the emptying to only once a year. The council offered an emptying service and Dad always arranged it once Peter had paid. This system worked well as long as we were on good terms with our neighbours, which Dad made sure he always was and I have always tried to do the same ever since.

As soon as they moved in Peter applied to the General Post Office for a telephone line. Mr Churchill had had one for years on the Westerham exchange, but now the village exchange was being extended and telephone poles were being erected all along the main road and down Well Street. It took ages for them to reach our cottages. We were the last to be connected, but eventually our neighbours got their telephone line which Peter considered essential in his line of work. I thought it would be very convenient to have our own telephone but Dad said it was a waste of money and would never catch on. I disagreed, but knew it was pointless arguing with Dad once he had made up his mind about something.

Dad bought a local paper every week to keep up to date with all the gossip, and I was really upset when I read that the cinema in Westerham was being closed down. I have some very happy memories of going to The Swan Picture Hall with Hank and my best friend Millie. Millie and her Mum moved up to Yorkshire after the war where they had family. We wrote a few times but Millie married an older man with young children and we lost touch. After Millie moved away I went to the pictures a few times with Dad, but it was very rundown. They changed the name to The Tudor Cinema and made a few improvements, but it just wasn't the same and closed down for good not long afterwards. It was demolished and a few swanky houses were built on the site.

In 1963 Dad was slowing up and working even shorter days on the farm, the hay cutting wore him out. The farm was also changing with fewer cattle and more sheep; Mrs Mann was at home a lot more now because she had retired, although she still made guest appearances and did some teaching in London and abroad. Dad made sure everything ran smoothly with the various cars and vans that came and went as well as maintaining the garden and farm machinery. The previous winter had been particularly hard with snow on the ground for months, and Dad said it had got into his bones. When summer eventually arrived, he didn't seem to have much energy and was having trouble with his leg. He lost interest in his music and would go to bed straight after a supper of cheese and cream crackers with a cup of Horlicks and listen to the news on his transistor radio.

On November the 25th President Kennedy was assassinated in Dallas. Dad took this shocking event very badly, the news coverage went on for weeks, what with the funeral and then the police investigations. Dad harped on about Pearl Harbour and how the Russians were a threat to our safety and kept quoting Mr Churchill.

"We are no longer safe in our island home."

In December, on Friday the 13th it had been sleeting all day and the wind was bitter. Dad arrived home with a lovely bit of scrag end from one of the old rams that had been butchered by Mr Allman who had an abattoir and a shop in the next parish. As he plonked the cardboard tray on my nice clean table it was leaking blood all down the side.

"You can make one of your lovely stews tomorrow, Joyce."

Mr & Mrs Mann only liked the finer joints of meat and gave their staff the poorer cuts. Dad always got extra because Albert didn't like lamb, he said he could taste the wool in it. I cooked the stew overnight in the bottom of the Rayburn and it came out succulent and tender for our Saturday dinner with parsley dumplings, home grown cabbage and boiled potatoes. Dad went off early to bed after supper as usual and I followed a couple of hours later after I had watched "That Was the Week That Was". I think David Frost is very clever and I love Millicent Martin, but Dad didn't really approve, he said they were disrespectful.

I fell asleep as soon as my head hit the pillow and woke with a start about 2am, but went straight back to sleep thinking a fox out in the woods must have stirred me. Dad was always an early riser and usually brought me a cup of tea in bed, but not this morning. I woke about seven and knocked on his bedroom door. No reply. As I opened the door I could see he was lying on his back with his mouth open. I touched him, he was stone cold - surely, he couldn't be dead? I tried to lift his arm; it was stiff. How could I not have known that Dad was in distress when I woke in the middle of the night? I had let him down badly. I went next door to ask Olive if I could use the phone. Peter was away again and she was in her dressing gown. The doctor came out straight away and said Dad had suffered a major aneurism and there was nothing I could have done. The doctor also explained that Dad would have been unaware and not suffered, but that was little comfort to me.

Dad's funeral was the day before Christmas Eve and a few friends and neighbours gathered to pay their respects: Mr and Mrs Mann, Albert, Peter and Olive and a couple of chaps from the farm. They were all very kind but I felt so lonely. They came back (except for Mr and Mrs Mann) for sherry and mince pies and some Christmas cake that I had made in September. I had busied myself on the morning of the funeral making pastry and baking the pies. Dad's coffin was in the parlour and the undertaker took him and me to the crematorium after I had made sure all the curtains were closed. Dad wouldn't have wanted a church service; he never went back after the Lefty vicar came with his mad ideas, even though he had been gone for years and by all accounts the new vicar was a good man and very musical.

Dad's ashes were laid to rest with his wife's, miles away in Sussex at the nearest crematorium on the 30th January 1964, the same day that Mum had died twenty-five years earlier. I left some flowers and one of Dad's cabbages on the grass next to the plot. It was such a long way to go I did not want to return. I wish now that their ashes had been scattered at home in the garden, but that sort of thing wasn't done in those days. I just followed the advice of the undertaker, and Dad would have wanted to be with Mum Peter and Olive asked me if I wanted to join them for Christmas lunch but I said no. They had all sorts of fancy things like prawn cocktail and baked Alaska with lots of wine and liqueurs. I just wanted a quiet day at home. I listened to the carol service from Kings College Cambridge while I roasted a pheasant that Albert had given me, with some of Dad's home-grown vegetables. I ate the rest of the mince pies with a schooner of sherry in the evening and watched "A Christmas Night with the Stars" hosted by Eamonn Andrews, then went to bed and had a jolly good cry.

The first thing I did after Dad died was to apply for my own telephone number. The GPO told me there was a party line available and I was delighted. At last I could ring people up instead of having to bother Olive or run back and forth across the fields with messages. I chose a two-tone green telephone and had a bell fitted by the front door so I could hear it ringing upstairs. My number was 331. I cycled down to Westerham and gave my new phone number to the haberdasher and put a postcard in the newsagent's window advertising my dressmaking and repair service. The card cost me two shillings for five weeks and I received half a dozen phone calls during that time with enquiries and got two nice little jobs from it.

Peter used the phone much more than I did and quite often when I picked it up he would be talking to a customer. I would carefully replace the receiver and wait a few minutes before trying again, but sometimes he was on the phone for ages. It didn't really matter, the convenience of having a telephone was so huge I couldn't imagine being without one now.

I was still working up at the farm which took me out of myself, and Olive asked me to make her some curtains. They were having so much work done to the cottage that I couldn't keep up, although the garden still looked like a bomb site. Albert had reared a few pullets and gave me three pretty little speckledies. I housed them in Dad's old shed at the side of the cottage and Albert fixed a nice high fence to stop the foxes getting in. I called them Maud, Flo and Rose and they all laid one delicious brown egg each at least every other day. I could watch them for hours scratching about in the run and chasing the butterflies without a care in the world. I let them run loose when I was tending the garden, they loved all the slugs and worms I dug up for them although they didn't always scratch in a convenient place and were a bit too fond of my spinach plants.

I also noticed a little chaffinch that picked up scraps the hens had missed, and started throwing him bread. I hung a bird feeder by my stable door just outside the kitchen and he became a regular visitor. I thought of Sir Winston sitting by his pond feeding the little robin and I started putting bread on the top of the door. It wasn't long before he was taking bread out of my hand, and he came for his breakfast every morning. This went on all summer and through the following winter. Spring came and went and still the little bird was a daily visitor, sometimes coming back for second and third helpings. Imagine my delight when one nasty wet morning in June he turned up as usual but with one of his offspring, he was teaching the fledgling how to gather his breakfast. I continued feeding them throughout the summer but when winter set in they stopped coming. I never saw them again.

The animals stopped me feeling lonely and I spent more time outside watching and listening to nature. I always took out slops for the hens before breakfast and one morning I saw something move in the ditch. I thought it was a rat to start with, they were a real nuisance and always trying to steal the eggs. As I approached I could see it was bigger than a rat as it disappeared into the hedgerow, perhaps it was an injured fox?

The following day I saw movement again but this time a little black and tan dog jumped out of the ditch, she was hungry and after the scraps. I found her a cream cracker which she took very timidly, her fur was matted, she was very thin and limping. She followed me indoors and drank a whole bowl of milk before settling herself in front of the Rayburn. She let me look at her front paw which had a deep cut in it and when I bathed it with salt water she whimpered a little, but made no attempt to move.

I told Albert and the post mistress but no one had reported a lost dog so I bought a dog licence and got her a red leather collar and lead. I made her a comfy bed with a pillow covered in towelling, and bathed her with flea shampoo in the old tin bath out in the yard and called her Sadie after a song Dad used to sing; "Sadie was a Lady." My new companion cheered me up no end, she followed me everywhere and gave me such a welcome when I got in from the farm. She was my very best friend.

Christmas in 1964 reminded me so much of Dad. Even now I don't like Christmas, it will always be a very sad time for me. I made a New Year resolution to stop moping about and was beginning to feel better with the help of Sadie who was such a loving little creature. Chartwell had been closed up for the winter and Sir Winston had retired from politics the previous summer. The Manns were out of the country and everything was quiet at home, even my next-door neighbours were holidaying abroad in Spain. Then came news reports on the television and radio that Sir Winston was unwell. There were crowds of reporters outside his house in Hyde Park Gate for several days, until on the 24th of January it was announced that he had died at breakfast time. I heard it on the one-o-clock news and it brought all my old sadness back in a huge wave of uncontrollable sobbing. The Queen decreed that he should have a state funeral and the crowds lined London's streets just like the Queen's Coronation with thousands queueing to pay their last respects in Westminster Hall. The BBC said that the queue was over three miles long at one point.

The service in St Paul's Cathedral was so emotional, and I will never forget watching the boat with his coffin making its way up the Thames to Waterloo Station where a train took the great Sir Winston Spencer Churchill to be laid to rest with his ancestors at Bladon. The flag at Chartwell flew at half-mast for many days and everyone was sad, the news affected the whole country and many people worldwide; it was hardly possible to believe that such a great man had gone for good.

In a strange way I think Mr Churchill's death helped me with my own grief, for after a few weeks I was feeling a lot better and looking forward to the spring. I had ordered my seed potatoes and decided to try growing a few different varieties of vegetables like tomatoes and courgettes. Dad always grew marrows, but they took up a lot of room and I never thought they tasted of much. I fancied going continental! Percy Thrower presented an excellent gardening programme on the TV and I was feeling adventurous. Albert helped me make a cold frame out of some old windows he had found up at the farm and my "Gardeners Delight" tomatoes were a great success. I took huge pleasure in watching them ripen on my sunny parlour window sill and made lots of chutney at the end of the summer. I have always loved runner beans. When they are at their best I often have a plate of beans all by themselves with lashings of butter, a luxury that was never possible during the war. I always cook with butter now; margarine and lard are very poor substitutes in my opinion although I do still like a bit of toast and pork dripping for tea on a chilly Sunday afternoon.

For years Dad did "The Spastics", the Saturday football pools in aid of charity. "The Fab Four" as it was called was collected from the post office each week and I carried on after Dad died. I liked guessing the results, it was only a few pennies a go and great fun watching the football results on the television and checking them off my list. One Saturday in May 1965 several of my numbers came up and it looked as though I had won quite a few pounds. I did not have to wait long to find out, I received a letter the following week telling me I had won a share in the "Four Week Highest Homes Pontoon" and that I would be receiving a cheque for £961.16.5d - an extraordinary amount of money.

Now you may think me silly and superstitious, but there were a pair of noisy magpies nesting in the mistletoe oak that year and they had just produced three healthy fledglings! I didn't tell anyone about my win although the post mistress raised her eyebrows and smiled when I paid the cheque into my National Savings account. This was my chance, I would learn to drive and buy a car. I carried on doing the pools until The National Lottery started but I never won more than a couple of pounds after that.

It took me nearly a year to get my driving licence. I had lessons once a week but had nothing to practise in and failed my first test. In April 1966 I passed my second test and went straight off with my driving instructor to buy an Austin A40 Mark II. It was smoke grey with a wooden fascia board, did 36 miles to the gallon and cost me £693. I drove it home with my instructor following behind and parked it in its new space that Albert had helped me make in the front garden. Dad would have been so proud of me and probably a bit jealous. He would also have been cross that I had pinched some of his vegetable patch but I didn't need as much space now and would never be as good a gardener as he was.

Soon after that Chartwell House and Gardens were opened to the public by The National Trust. Lady Churchill never came back after her husband died although she did visit with her daughter Mrs Soames to advise and help prepare the property for the opening on the 22nd June, and visited regularly after that. A lot of work was done to get Chartwell House back to how it was before the war, and they built toilets and a restaurant up on the north field. I thought of poor old Mrs Donkey Jack who wasn't even allowed to build a tiny shack on the common, but The National Trust had no problem getting planning permission. They also turned the old kitchen into a shop which I always thought was a terrible shame. Miss Hamblin was given the job as property manager, which was a very popular choice with the locals, she was such a lovely lady and so fond of Chartwell and the Churchills.

The house was open four days a week from spring to autumn which created an awful lot of traffic, it seemed like the whole world wanted to see where Sir Winston Churchill had lived and pay their respects. They even extended the route of the 706 from Westerham to save visitors a long walk up the hill. I wished they had done that years ago before I had a car, it is a very long walk to Chartwell up that hill from Westerham and not easy on a bicycle either, particularly when you are loaded down with shopping.

My other extravagance was the purchase of an electric sewing machine, a beautiful second-hand Bernina that not only did straight stitching but a variety of zig-zag and embroidery stitches. I had been told by Margaret Fleet from Evenden's that all the local schools used Bernina machines because they were so well made and she recommended her customer, a local repair man who worked for Surrey County Council who sold reconditioned machines. Dad always said that it was better to have something well made over fancy. I traded in my old treadle machine and was delighted with my purchase which enabled me to sew much more efficiently than before, earn more money and learn a new skill; free machine embroidery. I was still working a few mornings up at the farm but really enjoying my sewing business. Mrs Mann was also getting itchy feet and in 1967 she performed again at The Albert Hall, her first public performance for six years.

The 1960s was a decade of great change although I think on reflection most of it passed me by. My neighbour Olive was a great follower of fashion and she asked me to shorten her hemlines on several occasions. I was lucky to have good neighbours after Dad died but I didn't always agree with the way they went about doing things. I was content with my quiet life and my furry companion Sadie. I had independence with my little motor car and even drove down to visit Auntie Florrie on one occasion after Uncle Bert died.

I liked my television and the radio. I was absolutely gripped by The Forsyte Saga with Susan Hampshire as one of the stars, and was very surprised to discover that she is dyslexic and really struggles to read and learn her scripts. I think most people have difficult lives and make the best of what they have. I could never have watched "The Wednesday Play" if Dad had still been alive, he would have said it was immoral and a bad influence. I still feel emotional when I think about "Cathy Come Home" - that poor girl and what she had to suffer. There was a whole world out there that I knew nothing about, but I had no real desire to find out, I was content with my little house, my job up at the farmhouse and my sewing.

In 1969 Chartwell was buzzing with news about the arrival of a new statue of Sir Winston Churchill by the famous sculpture Oscar Nemon. It was going to be sited in the centre of Westerham, the preparation for which had been going on for weeks in the very middle of the green that is guarded by General Wolfe with his sword at the ready on the western corner. The white limestone plinth was delivered first and according to Margaret Fleet, it created a bit of spectacle when it was craned into position, with lots of fussing about from the parish councillors. Then the statue arrived on the back of a lorry with ropes tethering it and a sack over Sir Winston's head, a rather sinister sight and the sack was hastily removed once the statue was in position.

I was keen to see the unveiling on Monday the 7th of July, I parked my car outside where The Swan Picture Hall used to be and walked up to Evenden's to meet my friend Margaret who was watching from the pavement outside the shop. The town was awash with reporters, Pathe News and VIPs, including Lady Churchill with her children and grandchildren and of course Miss Hamblin. They were all seated on staging in front of The Tudor Tea Rooms facing out towards the green where the statue was covered with a sheet. Sir Robert Menzies, who used to be the Australian Prime Minister, unveiled the statue to applause from the crowd and invited the family to join him. It was all over in a few minutes and the crowd dispersed while some very fancy cars drove the guests of honour away.

Apparently, the plinth was donated by President Tito in honour of his friend Winston who helped Yugoslavia so much during the war. I thought Tito was a communist dictator? Dad would be turning in his grave; he would not have approved of a Lefty being allowed to honour the great Winston Churchill! Politics is a funny old business.

*****

THE 1970'S.

In 1968, my neighbour Peter applied for planning permission to build a one storey extension. The plans had to be submitted several times. I am not sure why although I think Mr Mann had some sort of say in the matter. In December 1970 permission was granted and building work went ahead with even more disruption for several months. The builders were very noisy with their radios blaring out on all different stations, but at least they finished most days at tea time.

When the extension was finished it made my parlour quite dark and shady, but I put a bench up against the new wall in the back yard and it was a nice place to sit in the afternoons before the sun set over the oak trees. Olive and Peter did a lot of the decorating themselves and when everything was finished Olive invited me in to have a look. It was all very swish with a huge lounge that had a York stone fireplace leading to a small office where the copper boiler used to be. The scullery wall had been knocked down to make a big kitchen and a lovely breakfast room, and now they had two toilets, one upstairs, one downstairs, and central heating. There was also a new room behind the old parlour that had been made into a guest bedroom for when Olive's mother came to stay.

The decor was all very modern like something out of Ideal Home Magazine. Olive told me they had gone up to the Daily Mail Ideal Home Exhibition at Olympia to get ideas and I must admit I was a tiny bit jealous. Olive asked me to make new curtains for all the rooms, some of the material came from Heals with big bold wavy lines in brown, mustard and orange. The fabric was very good quality but the pattern made my eyes go all over the place making it tricky to match up the lines. I stole some of their colour schemes to do a bit of painting at home, orange was the "in" colour. I liked everything they had done but what I really envied was their central heating. My cottage was cold and damp in the winter despite having the Rayburn that I kept ticking over constantly on a very low heat for my hot water. It was perfect for cooking casseroles and my favourite pudding, egg custard made with my own hens' eggs and a little bit of nutmeg.

When it was really cold I lit a fire in my bedroom before going to bed which just kept the chill off a little for when I rose in the mornings. My bathroom had an electric wall heater but it was very expensive and I tried not to use it. The Rayburn had to be stoked night and morning and de-clinkered every day. The sulphur fumes made me catch my breath and I had developed a very rosy glow on my cheeks from the extremes of temperature. I never did look after my skin very well, I have always been more interested in looking after my house rather than my complexion. Apart from all that I had gone down with bronchitis for the second winter running, and the doctor told me I should give up smoking. I knew this was a good thing not only for my health but also to save money, I was spending £1 8s a week on cigarettes, nearly as much as I spent on food. The first two weeks were a real struggle, but each day got a little easier than the last except I put on even more weight. Boiled sweets were the culprit, I tried dieting but every time I lost a few pounds I ended up putting on what I had lost plus a few pounds. I will never be a Twiggy.

Once their cottage was finished inside Peter and Olive turned their attentions to the garden and asked Albert to build some stone walls for them. He was now head gardener up at the farm and had just one chap to help him with general labouring tasks. Mrs Mann only needed Albert three days a week as her private gardens were fully landscaped and there were no more grand plans in the pipeline. Albert was always keen to earn a bit of extra cash and Peter was full of ideas for landscaping his plot with the help of Albert's stonemasonry skills and gardening knowledge. The project continued month on month just like Mr Churchill's, every time one thing was finished Peter or Albert would get another idea and they just carried on and on. Albert had a particular expertise and interest in trees and shrubs, he had learned a great deal from Mr Vincent, the head gardener at Chartwell House. I have a very old weigela in my back garden that Dad planted when I was a baby and Albert taught me how to summer prune it to produce profuse deep pink flowers every spring, year after year. It is still going strong.

On the 15th of February 1971 decimalisation was made compulsory and what a lot of fuss and bother that was! It all seemed far too complicated and confusing; 10 shillings was now 50 pence with a "p" not a "d", a shilling was 5p and there were 100 pence in a pound instead of 12 pennies in a shilling and 20 shillings in a pound, 7/6d was 37½p and ½ p was a penny. The half-crown and sixpence were no longer legal tender and I was in a muddle along with most other people. It was even worse with the weights and measures; the shops were all selling things in pounds and kilograms to help people understand. And as for converting inches to centimetres! I still think in Imperial and then convert it; a foot is 30 centimetres and a yard is a bit less than a metre. When I am baking I use my old Imperial scales and convert all the weights if I am using a modern recipe book. I think the local butcher got into trouble for selling pounds of mince instead of kilos and I am sure all the prices went up.

Miss Hamblin retired from Chartwell House as property manager in 1972 at the end of the season and in 1973 Jean Broome took over. The National Trust were advertising for summer season staff and I thought I might like to work in the shop for a couple of days a week and went off for an interview. It turned out I knew two of the ladies already, they lived in the village. I was taken on as an assistant and loved working in the old kitchen that was now a shop, but sometimes I was sent up to the restaurant where everything got a bit frantic. The weekends were the busiest but I didn't mind working, I had nothing to keep me at home. Most of the visitors were very pleasant and many of them foreigners, particularly Belgian and Dutch people who wanted to see where the great man had lived. I was very impressed by how many of them spoke fluent English.

I did find the standing quite difficult, I really should have lost weight, my ankles swelled on long hot summer days when I had been on duty for several hours. It was always a real scramble at the end of the day because so many visitors arrived late to see the house and gardens and then crammed in to the shop at the last minute just before cashing up time with queues down the shop and sometimes out the door into the hall. I worked there for two seasons but did not bother to reapply for a third year. I was getting too old for all that, my legs throbbed in the evenings after a full day's work and I decided to concentrate on my sewing business where I could please myself.

One day when I was in Westerham I bought a little paperback in the antique shop that had a second-hand book section specialising in books by and about Churchill. "Painting as a Pastime" by Winston S Churchill was originally published in 1932, but this was a reprint. I liked the colour plates in the back showing some of his paintings which mostly were in very bright colours and Mr Churchill had such an inspiring way with words.

"Just to paint is great fun.

The colours are lovely to look at and delicious to squeeze out.

Matching them, however crudely, with what you see

is fascinating and absolutely absorbing.

Try it out if you have not done so – before you die."

After reading the book I decided I should have a go at painting before I died and bought some watercolours from the art shop in Sevenoaks. My first attempt was a big muddy mess and I realised I needed a teacher. I read in the local paper that a lady in one of the outlying villages ran an art group, it was only a short drive out near Hever Castle and when I went along to my first lesson I discovered I knew one of the other students, one of my customers from up on the ridge. I enjoyed my afternoons once a fortnight pretending I was a Victorian lady of substantial means.

I was told I had the wrong paints and sent off to buy a few primary water colours: Aquamarine, Lemon Yellow, Scarlet, Prussian Blue, Cadmium Yellow and Cadmium Red. I learned that shadows are the combination of the colour of the object plus the complimentary colour and I painted a colour wheel for my own reference. Now all I needed to do was learn to draw! I started off with landscape but got very frustrated and then moved on to plant drawing. I was a little more successful at that and spent many happy afternoons at home in my parlour trying to paint wild flowers with moderate success. I also discovered that I liked drawing with pen and ink and filled a sketchbook with little scribbles. I would never make a botanical artist but I did slowly improve. I made some cards and sent a watercolour drawing of mistletoe to Auntie Rose for Christmas.

I had corresponded with Auntie Rose ever since Mum had died and she wanted me to go up and see her because in her words; she was too long in the tooth to start gadding about the country. She was five years older than Mum and now 86 years old but still reasonably fit with a good sharp brain. She always sent me a birthday card with a lovely long letter to go with it full of news about what she had been doing. She was no longer working at the bakery and had moved to a little cottage on one of the canals that fed the River Cam where she spent her days gardening and cooking. She earned a bit of extra cash by going fruit picking and told me all about the characters she met, how many pots of jam she had made and the flowers she had grown. I was a bit nervous about driving all the way to Cambridgeshire and told her I would think about when I could come but I kept putting it off.

In September I was very shocked to receive a solicitor's letter to tell me that Auntie Rose had died and her funeral was arranged for the following week if I wished to attend. She had suffered a stroke whilst gardening but no one was around and her neighbour discovered her several hours later, by which time it was too late to help her. She was taken to hospital but never regained consciousness. I did wish to attend but I was worried about driving all that way in my car and am ashamed to say I gave in to my fears. To quell my guilt, I rushed down to the Westerham florist and ordered a wreath through Interflora for my dear beloved Auntie Rose. The solicitor arranged her funeral. I don't know who attended and I really wished I had gone. Auntie Rose was the last of my family and I was now truly on my own.

A few weeks later I received another solicitor's letter telling me that my aunt had made a will and I was the sole beneficiary. I would be advised in due course of the value of the estate. I had been through the same thing when Dad died, although he hadn't made a will and it took months to sort out so I wasn't holding my breath. I was very surprised to receive another letter shortly before Christmas telling me I had inherited £869 and a cheque for that amount was enclosed. My little inheritance did lift me a bit from the Christmas blues, I went straight off to the post office to pay it in. The solicitor suggested in the letter that I should make a will of my own if I had not already done so, but why should I do that? I had no one to leave my money to, I didn't want to think about it.

What I did do was arrange for a local man to quote for central heating, he was recommended to me by one of the art club ladies and was a very helpful cheery chap with a wife and young baby. He said he could start work in the spring and I agreed although I had no idea how disruptive it was going to be, it was now my turn to be a noisy neighbour. Richard, the boiler man did a very good job and was very kind, he helped me move furniture and was a very tidy worker, which I have been told is unusual for plumbers. The upheaval spurred me on to do a bit of decorating again and when it was all finished I threw away all my old rugs and a man recommended by Richard fitted some carpets for me in the front parlour and the bedrooms. Olive had given me some velvet curtains that used to hang in her lounge. I dyed and altered them to fit my two bedrooms and splashed out on some Sanderson fabric for curtains and cushions in the parlour.

Olive always invited me around for a cup of tea when it was time for the annual cesspit empty. I told her all about Auntie Rose and the solicitor's letter; she was very sympathetic and pleased about my windfall but urged me to make a will to avoid the money from my estate all being used up in legal costs. I said it didn't matter, I told her I had no one to leave it to and why should I spend my money now on solicitor's fees when I may need it for myself? Olive tried to persuade me but I really didn't know anyone that I wanted to put in a will, neither Mum nor Dad made a will so I wouldn't either. Olive was quite insistent because she had been thinking about her own will, she had been unwell and was rather sensitive about it all.

Olive's doctor could not find anything wrong with her and she had turned to alternative medicine. She was seeing a homeopath who told her there could be bad energy in her house. She was reading a book about geopathic stress and got it into her head that the cottages were sitting on a black stream. She was worried about the oak trees because the book claimed that oak trees thrive in areas of negative energy and often take root along natural ley lines. It all sounded a bit silly to me, after all trees will thrive where their roots can reach a good supply of water and the trees on Well Street were growing next to a ditch fed by a natural spring. Albert told me a long time ago that oak, ivy and mistletoe grow over water veins and that is why they are prone to attract lightning. Albert's knowledge made sense of the ancient myth and Donkey Jack's predictions, but he didn't believe the old superstitions, he said

"it is all a load of old humbug".

I didn't tell Olive about any of it, I thought it best to keep all that information to myself.

Olive also told me she had found a water dowser to come and test the house and she would let me know what he found. The water dowser never came and Olive never mentioned it again, I think Peter probably thought it was all a load of rubbish and told her not to be silly. The homeopath was not able to help Olive very much but Olive thought something was working and carried on seeing him. I thought she seemed more depressed but maybe that was just me. Eventually after several months her GP diagnosed something called ME, an illness that had only just been discovered. A lot of people thought it was all psychological and just in her imagination. I wasn't sure what to think but I remembered how Mum had been and did my best to be supportive and neighbourly.

The following winter was lovely and cosy with my new oil boiler sited in the old downstairs toilet and radiators in every room, even the bathroom. Sadly, my lovely little Sadie developed fox mange, she probably caught it from sniffing about in the old orchard. Her ears were badly infected and she couldn't bear me to touch them. I took her to the vet and was told there was no cure, I tried desperately to help her but the poor little thing suffered dreadfully and the vet said I should have her put down. I agreed immediately. I didn't want her to be in pain, she had such a sweet nature and never turned spiteful. I didn't want another dog, Sadie was my one and only canine friend and she could never be replaced, and anyway I was beginning to get a few aches and pains myself and did not walk as much as I used to.

I did get some more hens though, this time I rescued them from the local battery farm, I bought four little brown hybrids for £2. They had spent the first two years of their lives in individual cages with no room even to turn around. The unfortunate creatures had no feathers on their heads or breasts and had trouble standing on solid ground because they had been reared on wire and their claws were curled. When I first collected them, they couldn't walk and had to be taught how to peck and scratch, but within a few days they settled down. Each hen laid one egg every day right through the year, even at Christmas. They were little treasures, I called them Andy, Pandy, Looby and Loo. Looby was as mad as a hatter and spent most of her time on the hen house roof. The old footpath up to Chartwell always has a large crop of blackberries and every year I gather some for jam. Miss Bird happened to walk by one morning and stopped for a short chat. I told her about my new rescue hens and she seemed very pleased when I told her their names.

I was now making a lot of curtains for a lady who had recently moved in to a big house with a lot of land on the ridge. Her husband worked in the City and she was not used to country ways. The farmer who grazed their fields offered them a bird for Christmas which they were delighted to accept; it had become very fashionable to eat local produce. When the cockerel was delivered it was alive and kicking and they were both shocked and horrified. Neither of them could dispatch the bird and even if someone else had done the dirty deed they said they could not have eaten him.

The lady of the house knew about my hens and asked me if I wanted him. They brought him around in a cardboard box that very afternoon. It had been snowing all morning and as we opened the lid he flew straight up the mistletoe oak. We tried everything to coax him down, but eventually gave up and he roosted there all night. The following morning, I awoke to loud crowing long before dawn and by the time I was dressed and ready with the chicken feed he was pacing up and down the hen house fence desperate to get in to his new harem. He was an extremely handsome creature, black and gold with great spurs and a vicious peck. I called him Sid. I wished I hadn't taken him on really because he crowed from before dawn almost to dusk and serviced the hens constantly, they were as fed up with him as I was.

Albert told me to raise Sid's roosting perch so that when he wanted to crow he couldn't stretch his neck out, but it made no difference he just jumped off his perch and marched around the hen house crowing to his heart's content. In the spring a mink got in, killed him and took all the eggs. I was pleased that Sid had done his duty in protecting the hens who all survived the attack, his demise was a blessing in disguise, we all settled back down to a bit of peace and quiet. I often see wild mink in the ditch, they are beautiful creatures but very vicious, one stood its ground with Sadie once, I had to shoo it away with a broom. There used to be a mink farm about ten miles away and Albert said some had escaped and there was a pair living in the stream just below the Chartwell lake. I bet they loved Sir Winston's fish and probably stole the eggs from the nesting ducks and swans, not to mention all the silly pheasant and partridge that nest on the ground where they have no protection from predators.

The National Trust was actively promoting the virtues of Chartwell House now, and visitor numbers were growing year on year. The large volume of visitors often caused traffic problems, particularly on Sunday afternoons when the world and his wife seemed to be out in their cars for a drive around our narrow country lanes. Mrs Mann told me that there was going to be a Son et Lumiere in August and she had been given some complimentary tickets. She had already asked Albert but he didn't want to go, he preferred to listen to German Military Band music in his shed.

I thought it would be a nice thing to see. I dressed in my Sunday best and walked up Well Street where I just happened to meet with Miss Lingstrom and Miss Bird who had also been given free tickets, we all walked along together and I sat next to them at the concert. The production was called "A Man and his House" and was written by John Julius Norwich. I enjoyed seeing the house all lit up, but found the show (if you can call it that) a bit boring, it was all rather intense with lots of Churchillian speeches and a choir that sang wartime songs. My Dad would probably have liked it but I favoured a bit of Glen Miller or a good film.

In 1976 my neighbours of fifteen years retired to Spain for the sake of Olive's health, and number 2 was sold again. I had got used to them both and was sad that they were leaving. They gave me a forwarding address and said if I ever fancied a Spanish holiday I would be very welcome, but I couldn't see myself ever travelling abroad. I certainly didn't fancy flying and anyway I didn't have a passport. The new people had two young children, he was a mechanic who owned a garage in Surrey and she was a cookery teacher. They redecorated the whole cottage again but didn't do any major building work. I think he was a good mechanic but a bit slap dash when it came to DIY. There always seemed to be lots of things going wrong in their house, not least when the boiler caught fire and the fire brigade had to be called to spray foam all over it. The remains of an oil-soaked carpet were discovered in the boiler house, a spark from the boiler had set the whole thing alight.

They also had a fire in the kitchen chimney which caused a terrible mess when a wooden beam over the Rayburn was set alight from sparks coming down the chimney. The firemen said it had been burning for several days and they were lucky it had not flared up at night when we were all in our beds. They got rid of the Rayburn after that. I got the chimney sweep in to clean my chimneys but he said I didn't need to worry because I did not have a wooden beam over my Rayburn.

The couple were kind neighbours and the children well behaved, although they could be a bit noisy out in the garden. Their father built them a sand pit and a greenhouse for his wife who made a vegetable patch that was bigger than the whole of my garden. He always had lots of cars on the drive and sold me a Morris Minor in part exchange for my old Austin that I had trouble starting in the winter. He said it was because I didn't use it enough and that I must drive my Morris more than once a week down to the shops. I did go out and about in the summer but I liked to stay indoors in the winter, especially now that my house was as warm as toast with no damp anywhere. I could sit and sew in the front parlour with no need for fires or extra blankets, I felt very lucky indeed.

Change was afoot up at Chartwell House because Mr Vincent had decided to retire and was moving away. There had been a lot of events to honour the Queen's Silver Jubilee and I think Mr Vincent was a bit tired of all the disruption. Albert was not a man who showed emotion but he told me that he was very reluctant to see Vic Vincent go, he had been a very generous teacher. I had been asked to make some bunting for the village jubilee celebrations and enjoyed using up all my fabric scraps. Bunting is more difficult to make than one would think, several ladies in the village had a go but it all got handed back to me to finish properly. I was talked into attending a tea party organised by the WI, and took along some finely cut egg and cress sandwiches, it took me straight back to the war and made me very nostalgic. I had a pleasant afternoon with a few people that I was on nodding acquaintance with but I have never been good at small talk and would rather have been at home sewing or drawing. The whole country seemed to be having street parties to celebrate the Queen's Jubilee but I didn't get involved in any of that, it was more for families really.

In December Baroness Churchill (as she was now called) died just a few days before the anniversary of Dad's death. She was in her nineties and had a very good life but it definitely marked the end of an era, I think I cried more for Dad than for her, or maybe for myself. The following year I was still doing a few hours up at the farm and Mrs Mann told me that she and Christopher were going away for a few days to Aylesbury. Mr Mann had recently been diagnosed with terminal cancer and they wanted a little holiday together. It turned out that they were going off to get married. All those years we had called her Mrs Mann and they weren't married at all, not that it mattered really but everyone was a bit surprised. Albert said it was humbug (his favourite expression) and I am not sure Dad would have approved, but I thought it was rather romantic. Christopher Mann died on the 11th December 1978 at the age of seventy-five and it brought loads of old memories flooding back again of Mum and Dad and the Churchills. I decided to cancel Christmas and just work through it like a normal day.

I always look forward to spring in the garden but summer is my favourite season because I love going to all the local fetes and fairs. The bric-a-brac stalls are a good source of fabrics and haberdashery and I usually manage to pick up some good stock items from days gone by, as well as a few ornaments for my little cottage. Boot sales were a new experience and I went to a few, it still amazes me what people throw away just because something has gone out of fashion. If there was a raffle I always bought a ticket, but never won anything with one exception. I attended a Christmas Fair at the school and my number came up. I was invited to choose a prize from a selection of items including a bottle of whiskey, a box of chocolates and a book called "The Illustrated Golden Bough" by Sir James George Frazer. I had no idea what the book was and chose it purely because it had a painting of mistletoe on the front with some lovely drawings and photographs inside.

I had never heard of Sir Frazer but read the introduction and discovered that he was a Victorian anthropologist who had written thirteen volumes called "The Golden Bough" about the history of myth and religion around the world, the golden bough being the mistletoe plant. My copy is a greatly shortened version and generously illustrated which made it an easy read. I was gripped. I could relate to something on almost every page and realized that a mistletoe oak was indeed very special. A whole chapter is devoted to Baldur and the Mistletoe and there is a photograph of a painting by Sir Edward Landseer called "The Sidney Oak" that was painted in 1845. The oak tree was planted in 1554 when Sir Philip Sidney was born at Penshurst Place just a few miles down the road from Chartwell and it is still there. My curiosity was awakened and I discovered all manner of interesting claims.

Everyone knows about the tradition of hanging mistletoe up at Christmas, but I didn't know that some people believed the berries could be used to find underground treasure. There is an old tradition to place a divining rod of mistletoe after sundown on the winter solstice and if there is treasure to be found underneath the ground the rod will move as if it were alive. That reminded me of Olive and her water diviner and I wondered if there was anything in it. When the water pipes were laid across the old orchard Mr Mann told Albert that the water company employed a dowser to check the land for unknown water courses before they started digging. I also read that in ancient times it was believed mistletoe flowers that bloomed in an oak tree at midsummer could induce prophetic dreams if they were placed under your pillow. I was quite tempted to try that but thought better of it and remembered Donkey Jack's words never to tamper with a mistletoe oak. It also reminded me of Betty Brown and the fairies that might snatch her children.

Sir James George Frazer explains in "The Golden Bough" how the oak and the mistletoe are intertwined with witchcraft. He talks of wizards and witches who believe that the cutting of mistletoe during a mystic ceremony can endow the participants with the magical properties of the thunderbolt. I was a little unsettled by this, particularly as there had been word from Albert that just this year on the summer solstice, witches had been meeting up in the woods on the hill where the old house had been demolished just before the war. He thought it was all very amusing and said that they were just a bunch of hippies dancing naked around a campfire. I don't know how he knew that but I thought it was all rather disturbing.

"The Druids worshipped a mistletoe bearing oak

above all other trees

in the belief that every such oak

had not only been struck by lightning

but bore among its branches

visible emanation of celestial fire."

Sir James George Frazer.

*****

There were now frequent events up at Chartwell including more royal celebrations, this time for Charles and Diana's wedding, but I didn't bother to attend any of them, it was always too busy up there. I did watch the Royal Wedding on my colour television though and what a spectacle!

I was mesmerized by Lady Diana's dress; they said it had a 25-foot train and a tulle veil of 153 yards. I couldn't even imagine what it would be like to work on such a huge scale. The dress was ivory silk taffeta with antique Carrickmacross lace embroidered with sequins and ten thousand pearls. When Diana arrived at St Paul's her dress seemed to go on forever, I think they had trouble getting it all out of the carriage, it looked very creased. The bodice had a frilled neckline like a Tudor ruff with large puffy sleeves and all the bridesmaids had a simpler version of the same.

The smallest bridesmaid was Clementine Hambro, one of Sir Winston's great-granddaughters. She looked so sweet, he would have loved to have been there. I hoped to get a glimpse of some of the Soames family, I am sure they were there but I never saw them. I was also rather surprised to discover that Sir Winston and Lady Diana were distant cousins, he would have been very proud to be linked to the next Queen of England.

Diana smiled sweetly throughout the ceremony but I thought Charles looked a bit nervous, I think he has always been a reluctant celebrity. The Queen looked very serious, I wonder what was going through her mind? Was she losing a son or gaining a daughter? The Duke of Edinburgh on the other hand appeared to enjoy the whole ceremony and got in the way of the Queen Mother a few times in his eagerness to see the royal couple drive away from the cathedral on their return to Buckingham Palace. The crowds were huge, the atmosphere must have been electric, but I am glad I wasn't there. I did think the Emanuels who designed the dress looked a bit out of place in their arty clothes but I loved seeing all the fashionable guests in their beautiful outfits and fabulous hats. It was certainly a day to remember.

I didn't work up at the farm any longer and was very content to be at home on my own, I could always keep myself amused. My state pension was plenty to live on with a little bit extra coming in from my sewing business and I was in good health apart from a few aches and pains. One sultry evening I decided to go for a late stroll up the lane. From the brow of the hill the starlit sky was crystal clear with a crescent moon and there was not a sound. How fortunate was I to have lived in such a peaceful place all my life! As I walked back down the hill I was startled by the sudden shriek of air raid sirens echoing around the valley. It was terrifying. Had the war in the Falklands started all over again, or more likely the Provisional IRA must have bombed Chartwell? The sirens were very close, reverberating back and forth, then search lights appeared over Chartwell manically waving around the sky making it as light as day.

As I ran back to my cottage Winston Churchill's voice wafted through the air:

"We shall go on to the end.
We shall fight in France.
We shall fight on the seas and oceans.
We shall fight with growing confidence and growing strength in the air.
We shall defend our island whatever the cost.
We shall fight on the landing grounds.
We shall fight in the fields and on the streets.
We shall fight in hills.
We shall never surrender."

I bolted all the doors and windows, had I gone mad? I turned on "News at Ten", nothing much was happening, they were interviewing Sebastian Coe. I made myself a Horlicks and sat and thought about it. I must have imagined it, there was nothing to worry about, and went to bed wondering if I was losing my marbles and had trouble getting to sleep. I woke very early having had a restless night and after breakfast Albert called around to give me some Victoria plums and told me about the Son et Lumiere that was being staged over the weekend. He grumbled about the noise from the rehearsals and asked if I had heard the sirens last night. I felt so silly when I told him, he said they startled him too as he was woken from a deep sleep and thought he was having a bad dream. We both had a jolly good laugh, it was Robert Hardy not Sir Winston. We were all safe in our island home and I was just a gullible old woman.

The mechanic and his family were wanting to move to a bigger house and the cottage was put on the market again. The couple that bought it were young, newly married and posh. They moved in on a cold dreary day in November, the same day that the previous neighbours moved out. There was a bit of a to-do when they arrived in their two cars and two removal vans. One van blocked the lane completely while the other was parked precariously up on Well Street. They arrived at dinner time and started unloading immediately, but it took until dusk to empty both lorries. The lane was often impassable in the winter but rarely closed to traffic.

One of the locals, an elderly lady who lived on the other side of the hill was a volunteer up at Chartwell. She always used the lane as a shortcut and was outraged to find the road blocked.

153

She jumped out of her car and demanded that the lorry be moved in order for her to pass. The removal men explained that they could not move the lorry whilst it still had furniture in it and she would have to go back the way she came. I could hear all the goings on and went outside to see what the problem was. The lady recognised me immediately from when I worked up at Chartwell, she had been a volunteer for years and was a rather self-important woman.

She complained to me that the men must let her through because she worked for The National Trust and was required to attend an important meeting up at Chartwell House. I told her there was nothing I could do about it and she would have to go back and drive the long way around. She marched off muttering under her breath, making a seven-point turn in her little car before she disappeared up the hill. The meeting was probably the end of season talk, I don't think they would have missed her, she wasn't exactly a VIP. After the removal men had departed I went around to introduce myself to the couple who were rummaging around in the dark, the previous owners had taken all the light bulbs and stripped the place bare. I gave them a couple of light bulbs to get them through the evening while they unpacked.

Robert was something in the City and his wife was already pregnant, they had a little boy. They were a very quiet family and kept themselves to themselves, I don't think they wanted to mix with the likes of me and that suited me fine. That winter was a very snowy one and everyone at the top and bottom of the hill were snowed in for several days. The tractor from the neighbouring farm came through with his snow plough to clear the lane in order to get hay to his sheep, but that built up drifts on our front gardens. Albert helped me clear a pathway to my car but I never saw hide nor hair of the neighbours, they never cleared their driveway and I think he stayed up in London. It was so cold the stream froze and when the melt set in there were icicles hanging off my guttering that almost reached the ground. Everyone lost electricity for several days but I still had my Rayburn for cooking and some warmth, I just sat it out until the milkman got through four days later. I always have a good store cupboard and my freezer was full so I cooked a few stews to save wasting the food and gave some to Albert and his wife who were all electric and only had open fires.

The snow brought all the local telephone lines down and they were not repaired for several weeks, we were always last on the list. I decided to apply for my own line, I didn't like sharing with my new neighbours; sometimes I would lift the receiver and there would be shouting or she would be crying. It was not always easy to put the phone down without them hearing and I hoped she didn't think I was listening. The GPO had just been changed to BT and they said I would have to wait until they had a spare line which could be several months. It turned out to be even longer after the disruption with the snow and I cannot tell you how pleased I was nearly a year later when they switched me over to my own private telephone line. I tried very hard to stay on good terms with my neighbours, they were always prompt in paying up when the cesspit was due to be emptied, but I was never invited in.

When their little boy started play group his father didn't seem to be there much. Our cottage walls are very thin and the child had an unhappy disposition. It worried me to hear him screaming and every night he cried himself to sleep. His mother just shouted up the stairs, she never went to comfort him. I felt so sorry for the little mite, it reminded me of Aunt Emma. I don't think his mother could cope because soon after that a French au pair moved in to look after him when his mother started going out with a chap who drove a Rolls Royce.

I was at home all the time now, Mrs Mann didn't like living in the huge farmhouse after her husband died, so she sold up and moved to Surrey. I was aware of lots of comings and goings next door and often the mother would leave her son for several days with the au pair. They had no means of transport and she would ask me for lifts to get the little lad to play group and home again. I didn't feel I could refuse, I wanted to remain on good terms with them all.

In the autumn there was a terrible robbery at Heathrow Airport. It was on the news and in all the papers, the robbers were violent and they got away with millions of pounds worth of diamonds and gold bullion. A few days later I was driving to Allmans the butcher in the next parish when I came up against a road block with armed police swarming all over one of the farms along the valley. They waved me down, asked me where I was going, looked in the back of the car and beckoned me through, it was very scary. On the six-o-clock news they said police were searching parts of Kent and South London for possible clues to the gang's whereabouts. I made sure all my doors and windows were locked tight and wished I had my little Sadie to keep me company. The following week my neighbour's au pair turned up on my doorstep with the little lad dressed ready for school. She was very agitated and explained in broken English that her mistress was in hospital with a broken head, she had been assaulted by her boyfriend.

I taxied the little chap three times a week for the next two weeks and told the play group leader, a retired headmistress that his mother was in hospital and I was not sure if the au-pair had any money or means of transport. She listened to my concerns but I don't think she ever reported it. I wasn't sure what to do for the best and was very relieved when one afternoon after I had brought him home there was a knock at my door. It was his mother. She thanked me for all my help and told me she was feeling much better. She asked if I could take her down to the village shop because she was not allowed to drive. She also asked to borrow some money because she had not had a chance to get to the bank. I offered to give her some essential items but she insisted on going to the shop. I gave her £10. She bought bread, milk and toilet rolls along with some tinned stuff and I drove her home. She came straight round the following morning to pay me back but that was the last time I spoke to her.

The au pair went back to France and my neighbour became a bit of a recluse. I think the little boy was sent to boarding school although he may have gone to live with his father. The following year the cottage was sold and I never saw her again. Several years later the chap with the Rolls Royce was found guilty of handling stolen diamonds from the Brinks Matt robbery and sent to prison.

The town council were very upbeat about the new ring road that was being built partly along the old Westerham railway line. The M25 was going to be the largest ring road in the country and encircle the whole of London. Most people thought it would be a really good thing and take much of the through traffic away from the A25 which was now grid locked most of the time through all the villages. They were building a junction at Bessels Green which was just far enough away for me not to worry about and I looked forward to the opening of the new motorway even though I had no intention of using it.

There was a bit of controversy about the junctions, people said that Prince Charles who resided occasionally at Chevening House did not want all the traffic coming past his doorstep, but I am not sure how true that was. People do say that since the motorway opened there has been more criminal activity in the area because it enables people who are up to no good to make a quick getaway. I thought there were probably plenty of crooks living in the area already and didn't think a new road would make much difference.

One morning as I was on my way to the town to see my friend Margaret in the hardware shop there was a man with a walkie talkie standing by the entrance gate to Chartwell House. It all looked a bit sinister but it turned out they were making a television film and he was there to coordinate the opening of the gates and keep onlookers at bay, or as Uncle Bert would have said; "gongoozlers". There was a lot of coming and going over two or three weeks. The main road was closed on and off for two days while they filmed Robert Hardy who was playing Mr Churchill again, going back and forth to Chartwell in a Daimler. It was a long time before the programme was shown on the television but it was worth the wait. I like Robert Hardy but it took me back to my scary moment a couple of years earlier, he is an excellent actor and was very convincing as Mr Churchill. The programme was called "The Wilderness Years" and now I understand why Mr Churchill was not featured in

King George's Silver Jubilee book that Dad had bought for Mum.

In 1983 I was delighted to have new neighbours, a divorced electrician called Darren and his young girlfriend, Sue. They were totally different to my last neighbour, a friendly couple with a good community spirit, always willing to rally round when needed. They immediately embarked on more renovations, the house had been neglected by the previous owners but I didn't think it was that bad although the garden needed a bit of attention. Darren gutted the cottage inside and out and fitted enough lights to illuminate the whole village with a state of the art, trip switch fuse box! This system was very sensitive to fluctuations in voltage and constantly tripped out throwing them into blackout.

Our electricity was supplied by overhead cables and it was not uncommon to have two power cuts a week plus a drop in supply on a Sunday lunchtime, and then surges of power when it all came back on. Sue told me she was frightened of the dark and felt safer when the outside was floodlit. I still don't understand, there is nothing to fear from the dark, the countryside should be dark to see starlit skies and allow the wildlife to rest. Why move to the country and then make it like a town? I would much rather walk at night in a dark wood than a crowded city street.

All seemed to be fine, my neighbours were friendly and I was enjoying doing my sewing and pottering about in the garden with my hens. I did start selling eggs at the gate with a sign and an honesty box but some kids who had been camping in the field across the main road smashed all the eggs and stole the box. I also had milk taken from my doorstep a few times, by walkers I think. The National Trust had recently published a circular walk from Chartwell that was very badly drawn and people were constantly getting lost in our little lane. Often in the summer when my kitchen window was open and I was stood at my sink, ramblers would walk up my garden path, stick their heads through the window and ask if I could refill their water bottles. I never refused but I did think they had a bit of a cheek.

There also used to be a lot of treasure hunt rallies organised by car enthusiasts and they were always stopping me when I was gardening out the front to ask silly questions like

"How many balls has Churchill got?"

One chap asked me the way to Chartwell and when I told him he said that couldn't be right because he had just been up there. His rudeness put me in a bad mood and I replied,

"Oh well, they must have moved it last night!"

I like getting the church magazine even though I never go to church anymore, but I did not like the lady who delivered it back then. She was very posh and quite bossy but what really annoyed me was the way she would march in my back door without even knocking, as though she owned the place. Who did she think she was? She could make quite personal remarks and now I was a pensioner she kept trying to persuade me to join her OAP club in the village. I think she had a nerve, she was older than me, what made her think I would want to go and sit in a hall with loads of old folk who I had nothing in common with and try to make polite conversation? I have always been happy with my own company and that was not going to change. I can't be doing with do-gooders who think they know what's best for other people. Live and let live is my motto and there are a few people in these parts who should learn that.

My neighbours were still decorating and having a new kitchen fitted by a local carpenter. They invited me in to have a look, the kitchen units were very well made but it was not to my taste. Shortly after that Sue stopped going to work and became rather withdrawn. At the weekends they would sit on their new patio complete with ornamental fish pond and bog garden, they always talked in hushed voices. What they didn't realise was that when I was sitting on my bench in the afternoon sunshine I could hear every word.

It seemed that Darren was a jealous character and didn't like Sue going anywhere without him. He was always a good neighbour to me, friendly and helpful but he obviously had a controlling side that he cleverly concealed. Sue became more and more withdrawn and one day I went around to give her some eggs and she answered the door with a walking stick. She didn't invite me in and when I asked her if she was OK she said she had arthritis and was waiting to go into hospital for tests. I was very sorry to hear that and wished her well.

Soon after that I heard Darren having a heated argument with his ex-wife on the telephone, she had stopped him seeing his daughters and he was very angry. One Sunday morning before breakfast there was a terrible racket with a woman shouting and screaming at their front door. It was Darren's ex-wife and it transpired that she had received a letter from their teenage daughters who were travelling in America; both of them had joined The Moonies. The letter said they would not be in touch again because they had found happiness and inner peace! Darren pulled her inside to stop her making a spectacle of herself but the shouting continued. His wife accused him of abandoning them all, I don't know where Sue was while all this was going on. After nearly an hour she left quietly and I never saw her at the house again. I didn't see much of Sue after that either, it was all very sad and rather unsettling.

I was beginning to wonder if a house could attract bad things. I decided to plant some sempervivums on the larder roof. One of the ladies at the art club had told me an old wives' tale, it was believed in some parts that houseleeks kept witches at bay. I didn't know if that was true but my plants have flourished and multiplied and it's good to know that witches don't like them particularly as my house is so close to the mistletoe oak.

The winter of 1986 brought heavy snow again and in January blizzards caused snow drifts so deep up by Chartwell House that they almost reached the top of the wall. I thought it was just our cottages that were cut off but it turned out the whole area was at a standstill. Sue had been listening to her transistor radio and told me that a state of emergency had been declared in many parts of the country, including our whole district. There were no trains or buses, everything and everyone was snowed in. This time Darren and Albert tried to dig us out but the snow just kept blowing back in. After about five days they tried again and did a great job along with some chaps who lived further up the lane. People were skiing down the hill and apparently the army were dropping food parcels across the hills. This time there was no electricity for three weeks.

Many years before Mrs Mann had given me a large chest freezer which I kept in the outhouse and I was always prepared for bad weather. I also bought myself a little generator after being snowed in last time to run enough electricity to turn on the central heating, run the freezer and a few lights. I was very well placed to sit it out, unlike my neighbour who was all electric with no generator despite being an electrician. Darren asked me if I could boil up kettles of water for Sue on my

Rayburn while he tried to get hold of a generator. I was more than happy to do that but also felt rather smug. I didn't attempt to go anywhere, it was five days before Darren could get out in his truck with Albert and when they did all the shops were empty.

Once the spring arrived, everything got back to normal with beautiful mild sunny weather. I did a lot of gardening and Darren finished landscaping his garden with a pergola and extended his patio again, much to the disapproval of Albert who was not included in the project. Autumn arrived rather too quickly and I was dreading another cold winter. On Thursday October the 15th it had been raining all day and I had been invited to a craft party by a lady from the art club who lived near the castle. I have never liked driving at night but I thought I should support her as she always recommended me to people for sewing repairs and dressmaking. By tea time it had stopped raining and while I was heating up a tin of soup I became aware of thousands of tiny fruit flies all swarming up against the window panes desperately trying to get into my bright warm kitchen. I stepped outside and there was an eerie silence, the clouds hung heavy and there were no birds, everything had gone to ground.

As I left for Hever the wind picked up and it had started to rain again, it was a bit blustery and I was very pleased to arrive in Pig Down Lane along with half a dozen other ladies who had all braved the weather. I bought a few bits and pieces but was very keen to get home and was the first to leave. The wind had really picked up now and it was raining heavily. The country lanes were alive with trees leaning and swaying like drunken sailors and as I drove slowly through the flooded lanes the trees loomed over me as though to block my way. When I got to the railway line three trees had fallen across the road and breached the stream, it was impassable. I was forced to turn back and go on a long diversion past the reservoir.

By the time I arrived home I was exhausted and in a bit of a panic. I made sure the hens were safely locked up, battening down their hatches and mine. I made my Horlicks and watched the window panes blow in and out with astonishing irregularity from the force of the gusts. I decided bed was the safest place to be and lay there listening to the wind, great gusts followed by waves of rain like God or even Odin was throwing giant buckets of water at the windows. I imagined I was at sea in a small boat and dozed off dreaming of shipwrecks and Vikings.

I was woken suddenly about 2.30 a.m. to the sound of high winds roaring like a pack of lions and tiles flying off the roof. The whole house was shaking. I switched on my bedside light but there was no power. I kept candles and matches in the bathroom cupboard, and was used to power cuts in the middle of the night so went downstairs to put the kettle on the Rayburn. There was something wrong; the inner walls were shaking and looked like they could blow in just like "The Three Little Pigs" story that Mum read to me as a child. I ventured into the parlour only to discover that a large oak branch had snapped off and landed on the window shattering the glass and it was now half way into the room. The whistling wind was trapped in the space with fabric, paper and thread swirling around like a tornado. I shone a torch outside and saw part of my cold frame fly past in mid-air, it was like films I had seen on the television of tropical storms. How could this happen in England?

I sat up hugging the Rayburn until dawn when the wind subsided and gingerly opened my stable door. The garden was a tangled mass of trees, tiles, pots and broken glass. The mistletoe oak was missing, it had been uprooted and flung over my garden and landed on next door's extension. We could all have been dead in our beds. I tried to get out into the lane but there was too much debris and I only had my slippers on. It was obvious we were cut off again, the lane was impassable as was Well Street. My next thought was for my hens, the fence was down but miraculously their house was still standing. They were happily scratching about amongst broken glass and smashed tiles without a care in the world. Darren appeared to check I was OK. No-one had been hurt but the devastation was shocking, no power, no phones and no way of getting out. Sue was not in a good place and I made her a cup of tea while Darren did a recce, there was a lot of damage to their house whereas mine was just a broken window and a few tiles off the roof. I did wonder if perhaps my houseleeks had protected me after all but I was very concerned about the mistletoe oak.

This time it took even longer to clear the roads and lanes and another state of emergency was declared. Several cottages including mine were without mains electricity for weeks and no phones for months. It was at least a week before any vehicles could get through, even the farmers were stuck. It said on the news that one man had died and one poor lady gave birth in the middle of it all. I was fortunate in that the damage to my cottage was minor, unlike number 2 that had major structural damage to the walls, windows and the roof. The disruption caused Sue's illness to accelerate, particularly after she discovered that Darren had no buildings insurance and little money to do the repairs himself. They moved away and the house was left in a terrible state of disrepair. The windows were boarded up and the extension roof was letting in water. The main roof had lost hundreds of tiles and those that were left were very unstable, they rattled ominously when it was raining heavily or windy. I often heard tiles randomly crash to the ground but I didn't venture around there for fear of injury.

The garden hadn't been cleared, patchy grass and nettles were growing up through uneven layers of tiles, bricks and broken glass. At night I could hear what I hoped were mice scurrying about inside and they were now in my roof as well. I think they were probably rats, there were certainly plenty in the garden. I had to call the council on several occasions, the rat man became a regular visitor. He was an amiable man and taught me a lot about keeping chickens including how to dispatch them when they were poorly by biting off their heads! Albert had not suffered too much damage to his cottage but the loss of several trees in his woods upset him deeply. He helped me get my garden ship-shape again and spent many months clearing and cutting his fallen trees which he sold as firewood, there was no shortage for years to come. The devastation was heart breaking, not least up at Chartwell where most of the woodland had been flattened in one fell swoop, the trees scattered like giant matchsticks all over the hill.

Everything gradually got back to normal after years of clearance and replanting, the sound of chain saws echoed through the valley for several seasons. One excellent side effect of The Great Storm was that many of the power cables and some telephone lines were replaced and re-routed underground. However, this was not a speedy process and as usual our little hamlet was last on the list, but I am grateful for small mercies. I still get the occasional power cut here but the service is greatly improved thanks to the hurricane and the army of men and women who worked so hard to get all the services up and running again.

Eventually after over a year of it standing empty number 2 was bought at auction by a property developer who had already purchased the fields and the old orchard from Mrs Mann. The new owner lived up on the ridge in a lovely old farmhouse with his wife. He had bought his small country estate many years previously and renovated the big house before selling it on and moving into the farmhouse. When Mrs Mann moved away her estate was split up and went to auction. The National Trust tried to buy Chartwell Farm but I think they wanted it too cheap. Anyway, the property developer bought some of the land including the old orchard and all the farm cottages that still had agricultural tenancies with sitting tenants. He paid off most of the tenants and applied for the restrictions to be lifted.

One nice old lady who had just lost her husband didn't want to move, she was much tougher than me but not in good health and was constantly hassled by her new landlord, but she stuck it out only to die a few months later. She was exhausted from the constant aggravation by her change in circumstances. I felt very lucky that I was secure in my own home with no landlord to worry about. Mrs Mann would have been furious and Albert was really cross about it all, he hated seeing the estate broken up and was angry that this chap was riding rough shod over everyone. He got even angrier when the developer sold off the houses at a huge profit and it made him determined to get the restrictions lifted on his own cottage. He eventually got what he wanted after a long drawn out argument with the council and expensive visits to a solicitor, but he said it was worth it because now his house had tripled in value, as had mine.

The property developer immediately started work on number 2 and I had to put up with another six months of builders' noise and disruption, but at least the house was being made habitable again, the damp had got in and I was worried about my walls. The cottage was stripped and fitted out with the best of everything, the property developer told me that the house was to be a holiday home for his son's family and they would only be there a few weeks during the year. That was fine by me, it was lovely to have a bit of peace and quiet. Although I didn't like the ruthless tactics of the new owner I found him a pleasant enough chap to talk to and wanted to keep on the right side of him.

He fancied himself as a bit of a farmer, each spring he would buy a few young bullocks at auction to be fattened up for the winter and then sold the meat to his friends, half a cow or a quarter all butchered to order. He gave me the offal: kidney, heart and tongue, all the bits other people didn't want. This was the first and last time that I boiled a tongue. It had to be skinned and the texture was that of a human tongue but fifty times bigger. I never bought or ate tongue again after that.

The new owner grazed livestock on all his fields, including the old orchard behind Mistletoe Cottages. The cows were always escaping usually because there was not enough grass. His housekeeper Tammy was a keen horsewoman and she helped him out in return for keeping her horses in the fields with his cattle. She had a couple of magnificent hunters that she rode in dressage events, but also owned a vicious little Shetland pony who kicked and bit anyone within stroking distance.

I loved seeing the cows back in the fields, they are such gentle creatures but I never went near the horses. I have always been nervous of horses apart from Mr Sykes's big old Shires. One day the cattle were being walked up past Chartwell to fresh grazing. Tammy was at the front carrying a bucket of nuts and a couple of lads with sticks were bringing up the rear to chivvy the silly animals along and stop them diverting into the car park at Chartwell. All the gates had been shut and some National Trust members were rambling along the main road with maps in hand. As they stepped back to let the cattle through, they threw coins into Tammy's bucket and asked what charity she was collecting for? Tammy thought it was hysterically funny and delighted in telling everyone the story, several times over.

The farmers often used to move their livestock along the lanes but it happens less and less now because there are too many cars and most people don't know what to do when they meet a herd of cows or a flock of sheep in the road. The whole beef enterprise came to a very sharp halt when mad cow disease reared its ugly head and restrictions were brought in to stop the movement of cattle. It was no longer possible to buy cows at auction and the local abattoir was nearly shut down. Cows are never seen grazing in the fields these days, it is such a shame.

*****

Once 2 Mistletoe Cottages was finished inside and out it was kept very spick and span. Albert was paid to keep the garden neat and tidy and the property developer asked me if I wanted to clean the house every now and then when his son wasn't there. I didn't want to go back to doing cleaning so Tammy came in once a fortnight instead and always popped in to see me before she left, sometimes with a bunch of flowers, she was quite thoughtful.

It was very different when the family were staying there, I found them stand-offish and unfriendly, particularly the daughter-in-law. The children were very boisterous and their parents argued constantly. It seemed they had a passionate relationship and were very noisy at night in the bedroom, I moved my bed so that it was not against the party wall. They struck me as two very selfish characters. He was an only child who had been spoiled rotten by his mother because he was diagnosed with cerebral palsy when he was born. His father never really came to terms with the disability even though it was very slight, and pushed him hard to be sporty and fit. The son was not competitive at all and much more interested in computers, he worked as a computer analyst but had recently lost his job, which annoyed his father. The wife seemed to me to be a bit of a floozy, she was much younger than him and always done up to the nines, a terrible flirt. I was very pleased they didn't live next-door all the time.

Their permanent address was up in Norfolk somewhere and that very first summer the family stayed at number 2 for the whole of August and returned back home after the bank holiday to get the children back to school. The grandparents immediately left for their Spanish villa in order to have a rest after entertaining their grandchildren for over a month and I was delighted to get the place back to myself. While they were away I was very surprised to get an international phone call from Spain; it was the property developer. He said he had been trying to contact Tammy and needed me to get a message to her.

"I have something shocking to tell you,
our son has been murdered and the papers are sniffing around.
Don't say a word to anyone.
We will explain when we get home."

I couldn't believe it. Tammy's horse was grazing the field opposite and I found her grooming him up near the gate. She was so shocked when I told her the news that she burst into tears and then so did I. She immediately drove back to the farm where there were already reporters waiting outside. I walked back down to my cottage and made a cup of tea. I was exhausted and immediately thought of the mistletoe oak.

"Tampering with a misteltein oak could bring sickness or even death to those who did not respect it."

Over the next few days reporters turned up at number 2 and on my doorstep; but I didn't speak to them. Albert wanted to know what was going on but I said I didn't know, I thought it best as he could be a bit of a gossip. The property developer came around when they returned home from Spain to update me. He said his daughter-in-law had found her husband dead at home and she was helping the police with their enquiries along with three men. The inquest revealed that because the victim had been born with cerebral palsy the death was not considered suspicious. But then a pathologist found strangle marks around the victim's neck suggesting that he had been asphyxiated or suffered blows to the neck. The cerebral palsy was very mild, he had a slight limp but he had been able to lead a normal life. He was a good swimmer; his father installed a swimming pool in one of the barns specifically for his son to learn to swim and exercise. I think that is how he met his wife because she was some sort of therapist.

I felt very sorry for the whole family, nobody deserves to see their child die and I worried for the poor children however unruly they might be, they had lost their father. The three men were put on remand but the wife was allowed to return home to her children, the trial wasn't for another six months and the newspapers lost interest. All the waiting took its toll on everyone, including Tammy who kept me informed of events as they unfolded.

When the trial started the parents stayed up in Norfolk and attended court every single day. All sorts of shocking revelations came out about their daughter-in-law's infidelity; how she had been having an affair with one of the accused men and that she was promiscuous, with a huge sexual appetite. One of the men had been a lodger in the family home and according to the prosecution had a jealous and possessive nature, he wanted her all to himself. The whole gruesome story was like something out of an Agatha Christie novel. There was even more intrigue when the trial was halted because a witness statement had gone missing and the judge said there couldn't be a fair trial.

The trial resumed a month later but although all the defendants were discredited, many witness statements were proved to be untrue and there was not enough evidence to convict the three men on remand; they were all acquitted. The judge in his summing up stated that as a witness the victim's wife was

"not only a proven liar
but wholly feckless and utterly immoral".

She also stood to gain financially from her husband's death as there was a life insurance policy. She was never put on trial due to lack of evidence but her father-in-law became obsessed with searching for the truth and spent many thousands of pounds on private investigators, without success. I visited their lovely old farmhouse on one occasion, they had photographs of their son and his children but their daughter-in-law had been removed from all of them. They eventually sold all their property in the area, the farmhouse, the cottages and all the land and moved away to make a fresh start. I still wonder if that was ever possible, could they ever have been happy again and did they see their grandchildren who were still with their mother?

I had my own worries over that winter, I was jittery about losing the mistletoe oak and there was a lot of trouble with the West Kent Hunt. I had learned to live with them over the years and although I didn't particularly approve of their activities it had always been part of living on a country estate. The National Trust was pro-hunt and encouraged meets in the car park up at Chartwell House. Some people enjoyed the spectacle but I was not one. The hunt was capable of causing a great deal of disruption when they were blowing their horns and whistling on their horses, galloping around the narrow lanes with a pack of hounds and followed by a convoy of four by fours also hooting their hooters and shouting. It brought back good and bad memories of when the Canadians were camped up in the woods. The soldiers were long gone and so were the trees, Chartwell had lost seventy percent of its trees in The Great Storm.

The Master of the Hunt was always polite but some of the followers were extremely arrogant and disrespectful to private property and the local residents. I didn't like their attitude and just stayed indoors, but Albert always got very agitated particularly when the hounds were loose. One year the hounds ran riot through his garden and caused quite a lot of damage to his herbaceous borders and vegetable plot. He was very angry. They offered him compensation but what good is that when the damage has already been done? In my opinion a lot of unnecessary anxiety for all concerned for a few so-called gentlemen and gentlewomen to have their sport.

The season that followed was very distressing with hunt saboteurs causing a lot of trouble. At one meet they brought their own dogs to confuse the hounds and one of the dogs got caught in a gin trap in the woods, it howled for hours. The hunt denied it was their dog and the saboteurs denied it was theirs. The police were out in force but just stood passively by. Albert watched the whole thing and said it was all a bit pathetic because all three parties were filming each other for evidence.

The next meet brought The Animal Liberation Front out again. The hunt tried to keep their dates secret to avoid conflict but the ALF always found out, it was thought they had an informer. This particular day the hunters were out in full strength blocking the lane in all directions and the hounds were in chase. I looked out my parlour window and could not believe my eyes, there was what seemed like an army of men marching up the old orchard dressed in black with balaclavas and they were waving baseball bats in a threatening manner. They were chanting something but I couldn't hear what. I bolted my doors and windows and went upstairs to peep out of the bedroom curtains.

Now that I think about it there were probably only a dozen or so men and some of them were probably women but it was terrifying all the same. The hunters stood their ground ready for conflict with some of the horses rearing up when both sides were shouting abuse at each other. Eventually the police arrived and dispersed everyone after a few scuffles and a couple of arrests. That experience will stay with me for the rest of my life and I worried again about the power of the mistletoe oak.

My new neighbours moved in on a blisteringly hot sunny day in August. They were a young couple and liked to party. The very first weekend they had a house warming in the garden with a ghetto blaster blaring out, strong language and raucous behaviour. The noise continued late into the night and I hoped that this was a one-off, but unfortunately it was not. Every weekend there was either a party or they would arrive home late and play loud music long into the night with the addition of noisy bedroom activity. I am no longer an innocent spinster!

They seemed to have plenty of money, he was a scrap dealer in South East London and she was studying a correspondence course on interior design. She redesigned the cottage and had decorators in, every room was changed again, a new kitchen and bathroom, designer paint, wallpaper and curtains throughout, even in the nursery ready for their new baby that arrived eighteen months later despite their abusive relationship. The noise did subside a little after that, certainly when the baby was tiny although the little thing seemed to be able to sleep through almost anything.

The mother then turned her attention to the garden and money seemed to be no object. She employed a professional designer and together they created a beautiful garden with a lovely choice of planting; roses, wisteria, crab apples and cottage garden flowers, it was beautiful and very romantic. She invited me around for coffee one morning, it was cess pit time again. The garden was blissful, the baby was playing in her playpen and I complimented her on how she had regained her figure so well after the baby. I discovered soon afterwards that her slim figure was largely due to her cocaine habit supplied by her husband who was also a user and a drug dealer with a conviction for armed bank robbery. He looked and was an aggressive extrovert who loved to flex his muscles out in the garden in full view of Well Street in the company of his undesirable mates accompanied by extremely loud music. His wife and child often went away overnight and he would have unruly drinking sessions with his unsavoury friends, the language was unspeakable. I have learned words that I never knew existed. I didn't dare complain, I was terrified I would get a brick through my window.

My neighbours' relationship seemed to go downhill from that point, whenever they were together they were not just arguing but fighting. He particularly was on a very short fuse, constantly hyped up with cocaine and aggressive not only towards his wife but his baby as well. His wife also had a foul mouth on her and could match his language, she always put up a fight and would scream at him phrases such as

"I am not your f***ing whore,"

and worse, with the poor little baby witness to it all. My walls were so thin I could hear every word and blow when things got nasty, usually late at night. He had recently acquired a brand new American pick-up truck which he left standing on the front drive running for hours on end with all the fumes seeping through my kitchen window. I was too scared to say anything.

Around the same time there was a lot of coverage in the local news about a mother who had gone missing, her car had been found at a shopping centre in Essex and she had not returned to collect her children from school. There was a big police operation to find her but she didn't turn up. My neighbour was becoming more and more aggressive. I was frightened to even go into my garden when he was there. When his wife was out he left the baby in her play pen for long periods even though she grizzled and cried. The rows were now daily and Saturday nights always the worst, sometimes he would come home and throw things, I could hear the sound of breaking glass and even furniture upturned and thrown against the walls.

One evening when they were all out, a strange car was parked on their drive with two men sitting inside, they looked quite sinister. I was so worried about it that I rang Albert and asked him if he could find out what they doing. Albert walked down the lane with his overcoat on to make him look bigger and a large walking stick hidden underneath. He knocked on the passenger window, the chap wound his window down, showed him ID and told Albert to go back home and lock the doors. They were plain clothes police detectives.

The following December I was suffering from my Christmas doldrums which were worse than usual. I was unhappy and scared and for the first time in my life I wanted to leave my little cottage, but did not know where I could go. My neighbour had been absent all week and on Christmas Eve his wife left the baby at home with him while she went shopping. I think they were already estranged by then because I heard them shouting at each other, she did not want him there on Christmas Day. The wife arrived home about five-o-clock only to discover that he had locked her out and had the baby inside with him. She started shouting and crying and he just shouted back a tirade of abuse with his daughter screaming in the background. I thought I should call the police but I was frightened and while I was thinking about it I heard the wife call 999 herself, from the front garden on her mobile phone.

By the time a squad car arrived the father was smashing up the house, throwing furniture at the windows and yelling at the baby who was screaming with terror. He opened a bedroom window and shouted to the police that he had a father's right to see his child on Christmas Day and no one was going to stop him. The disturbance went on for several hours by which time two more police cars arrived. The police thought he may have a gun, they made the wife wait in her car out of sight up on the main road. A policewoman came around to my cottage and told me to stay inside, lock the doors and close all the curtains. I was petrified. Eventually he seemed to tire and got very impatient with the baby who was sobbing uncontrollably. The police negotiator managed to talk him into opening the door and hand the baby over. They swooped in, handcuffed him immediately and bundled him into the squad car which drove off.

The policewoman went inside with the mother and after about half an hour they left the house as well. It was nearly midnight when most children would be asleep in bed with the anticipation of Father Christmas coming down the chimney. Would that poor little mite remember the events of that day? No child should have to experience such violent trauma but I tried not to think too much about that; I had peace and quiet on Christmas Day and felt a little safer in my bed.

In January the mother and her baby moved away. She told me she was selling up to start a new life in London because she didn't like living alone in the country, the house was too isolated. The estate agent put a "For Sale" sign up and the cottage received a lot of interest from potential buyers. The national news had now picked up the story about the woman that had gone missing two years earlier. Her body had been found buried under a shed in a garden not far from where my violent neighbour operated his scrap metal business. He was implicated in her murder along with two other men and at the trial it was suggested that the murder was a contract killing done purely for monetary gain. At his trial my neighbour denied murder but did admit to burying the body, and it turned out the victim was his wife's stepmother; I cannot tell you how shocked I was. He was on remand but I still did not feel safe, I wanted to know when he would be behind bars permanently.

The following summer I bumped into the wife one day whilst shopping in Westerham. She was painfully thin and told me how unhappy she was and that she wished she had never moved away from the cottage. I said I was sorry to hear that, but I really, really, wasn't sorry she had gone.

During that period was the only time in my whole life that I ever wanted to move house, forced out by bad neighbours who not only made me unhappy but also fear for my safety. The mistletoe oak weighed heavily on my mind with all the things that had happened since it was uprooted by the wind on that dreadful night in 1986. My friend Albert was now very unwell with terminal cancer and had been admitted to hospital. Evenden's, the hardware shop was closing down so that it could be sold and my friend Margaret was being forced to retire. The shop was her life and she did not want to leave it. That mistletoe oak tree had a lot to answer for.

The "For Sale" signs went up again for 2 Mistletoe Cottages, it was described as a well-presented cottage with a large garden that had great charm. I thought it was over-priced but plenty of people came to look. The signs kept going up; "For Sale", "Under Offer", "For Sale", "Under Offer", "For Sale", again and again. There was obviously something amiss. I wondered if a house could hold the memories of its residents and if so what terrible memories that house carried within its walls. I was also now convinced that the cottage attracted people with secrets to hide.

Someone told me once that we are often drawn to a particular place that fulfils what we are lacking in ourselves; I worried about what I was lacking in myself. Every now and then a stranger would turn up asking questions about the previous residents and their whereabouts. I had nothing to tell them, I had no idea where they all were but the remoteness of my little house started to bother me just a little bit. I was nervous about who the next residents might be.

The cottage remained empty and I was enjoying the solitude, I kept myself to myself and didn't venture out on foot or in the car on high days and holidays. Chartwell House was getting busier and busier. One of the ladies who works in the visitor centre told me that it is the most popular National Trust property in the country and on an August Bank Holiday they welcomed thousands of visitors. I can fully believe it and am very glad I don't work there anymore. The traffic on the main road is ridiculous on a Sunday with everyone tearing about and getting lost.

One very dreary Sunday morning I turned on the radio to listen to "Desert Island Discs" whilst cooking my dinner and there was a news flash. Diana was seriously injured, presumed dead. I immediately turned on the TV and the horrific story was unfolding of a terrible car crash in Paris. I forgot about cooking my dinner and just watched for hours. All that trouble between her and Prince Charles, their divorce and now this! I never did understand what she saw in Dodie but what a terrible tragedy! I couldn't stop watching. There was a lot of upset with the Queen and it was all so sad, I felt sorry for all the princes, Diana's boys William and Harry and even their father Charles. They all had to put on brave faces in such difficult circumstances.

I had a funeral of my own to go to. My good friend Albert died at home after a long spell in hospital. It was a very sad day. The service was at the same crematorium as Mum and Dad's and I went to see them while I was there. That will be the very last time I visit any of them, it is a very long way to drive. The roads are getting busier and busier, some days it is like living on a motorway even on my little lane. One day there were huge traffic jams all around the lanes with impatient drivers trying to find short cuts. It turned out that two lorries had got stuck on a bend up on the main road and blocked it for nearly an hour while they untangled themselves. If that had happened twenty years ago everyone would have got out to help, but not these days, people are always in so much of a rush.

When the doors closed for the final time at the hardware shop there was a presentation in the church hall for Margaret's retirement which I attended. I stayed for the party afterwards to support my friend. She was overwhelmed by the kindness and generosity of people and had no idea how fond her customers were of her. There was lots of reminiscing about when she started working there in 1944 and how they kept No 8 batteries under the counter for people's bicycles and torches during the blackout years. She also talked about the lovely smells in the shop of putty, methylated spirit, turpentine, linseed oil and paraffin that all used to be poured into the customers' own containers, and Mr Goose who did all the metalwork repairs.

Margaret knew almost everyone in the town and all the big houses had accounts at Evenden's, she was a fountain of knowledge. I wrote in the book that was presented to her along with a collection, and she had tears in her eyes. What was she going to do with herself? She said she wanted to take up fishing again and she liked a bit of gardening, but I don't think she really knew. I felt very sad for her, she had lost her purpose in life and all her knowledge was going to be lost for ever.

Eventually the sale of next door went through successfully and my new neighbour came around to introduce himself, a single retired gentleman who currently lived with his mother and also owned a house in Hampstead. He was friendly enough and keen that I should be a key holder for him because he would frequently be away. I was very pleased hear that and readily agreed to his suggestion. He invited me around for a cup of tea and was very proud of his furniture, lots of stainless steel and glass that did not really fit with the décor of the house so unfortunately it was all change again.

He was a night owl and seemed to like starting work when everyone else was packing up for the day. One night about eleven-o-clock I was woken to loud banging, he was hanging pictures and one had fallen off the wall. I suffered endless evenings listening to him stripping wallpaper with a scraper and sanding woodwork, so I turned my television up to drown out the noise and he had the cheek to come around and tell me my television was too loud. I was very cross and told him about his scraping and banging, he said he didn't realise the walls were so thin and apologised. He was a bit more considerate after that.

After a few weeks he started bringing his friends back to the cottage for weekends, and often introduced me to them. They were always beautiful young men, a different one every time and usually quite affected in their mannerisms. I didn't like the atmosphere, the bedroom noises started again and I decided to move into my old bedroom away from the party wall. I thought I should be grateful for small mercies, after all he was usually only there a couple of days a week and hopefully he wasn't a drug dealer or a murderer.

Fortunately, he only stayed for that one summer and then decided to move back to Hampstead because he said he missed the night life! Number 2 Mistletoe Cottages was put in the hands of a letting agent and the first tenant has just moved in. I have also read in today's paper that my previous neighbour has been given seventeen years for conspiracy to murder and armed bank robbery. I am having a schooner of sherry in celebration and hopefully I will sleep well tonight.

"Do not let us speak of darker days."

WSC

*****

EPILOGUE

Two months later on the 11th August 1999 Joyce wrote:

I am now up to date with my journal and today have witnessed the total eclipse of the sun. Chartwell was 97% on the line of totality. Special viewing glasses were issued by all the newspapers and there was a lot of publicity about not looking at the eclipse with the naked eye. I walked up to Well Street just clear of the oak trees. It felt very eerie standing there alone where the mistletoe oak had once stood. I watched the moon block out the sun through a cloudy sky, complete darkness fell and there was a sudden chill in the air just for a few moments before a bright crescent appeared and in no time at all it was done.

I remembered my mother on the scullery floor screaming at me and Donkey Jack talking of bad omens. I thought about Hank and wondered if he was looking down on me along with Mum and Dad, hoping that they didn't know about all the things that have happened since their passing; it would have worried Mum to death. There has been a lot in the papers about Nostradamus and his predictions of Armageddon. People are worried that the millennium will bring chaos and destruction with all the computers in the world shutting down. I am a little bit nervous, after all Donkey Jack was right last time when I was only five years old and scared of the solar eclipse, but I am old enough and wise enough now not to believe in superstitious nonsense.

*****

ENDWORD

On Thursday the 12th August 1999 Joyce Baxter was found in her kitchen by Richard, the milkman. He never arrived much before 10.30 am and today he was late. Joyce had slipped on the quarry tiled floor whilst making her bedtime Horlicks and been lying there all night in agony with a fractured hip, unable to reach the phone. Richard rang for an ambulance which arrived within half an hour and Joyce was taken into hospital. No one visited her and she was never well enough to return home.

An assessment was carried out on her mental health. She knew her name and what year it was but when asked who the Prime Minister was she replied "Mr Churchill". Joyce died intestate on the 2nd January 2000, she was cremated and her ashes were buried with her parents in Sussex. The cottage was advertised as attractive with potential for improvement and after it was sold the proceeds from her estate were eventually divided up between dozens of cousins both at home and abroad. None of them had ever met Joyce apart from her cousin Wilf who was not in good health himself. They received just a few pounds each.

ACKNOWLEDGEMENTS

I have lived very close to Chartwell for nearly forty years and always been interested in its history and its residents. The inspiration for my story stems from my own experiences and records from my own private archive. The full bibliography appears below but there are two publications that have been invaluable to my research.

The first is "Speaking for Themselves", the personal letters of Winston and Clementine Churchill edited by Mary Soames and published in 1998. I purchased a copy from the Chartwell shop when I was working for The National Trust as a visitor services assistant and Lady Soames very kindly signed the book for me.

The second book is Stefan Buczacki's first edition of his biography "Churchill and Chartwell", the untold story of Churchill's houses and gardens, published in 2007. The research carried out by Mr Buczacki is astonishing and really brings to life how the Chartwell Estate functioned when Winston Churchill lived there and also after he died.

The life of Eileen Joyce is well documented on the internet, but I also learned a lot about her from first experience by talking to neighbours and referring to personal papers in my possession. The Manns were respected members of the community and always philanthropic towards their staff and tenants.

Another very helpful chap was Bob Bailey at "Brooklands Transport Museum" who provided me with information on different modes of public transport in use both before and after WW2. In addition to the bibliography I found a wealth of information online including the BBC archive, newspaper reports and magazine articles that are too numerous to mention.

Lastly, I cannot thank Kev Reynolds enough, not only for helping me source local information in the beginning but also for his support and advice when the book was completed. I am indebted to his skills and generosity in editing the final copy to make it a better read by questioning a few facts and sorting out my punctuation. His encouragement throughout has been extraordinary and he has given me the confidence to continue writing.

BIBLIOGRAPHY

The Silver Jubilee Book.

The Story of 25 Eventful Years in Pictures.

Odhams Press Ltd.   1935.

The Mammoth Wonder Book for Children.

Edited by J.R. Crossland & J.M. Parrish

Odhams Press Ltd .   1935.

The Book of Good Housekeeping.

Compiled by Good Housekeeping Institute.

Gramol Publications Ltd.   1944.

Painting as a Pastime.

Winston S. Churchill.   1932.

Penguin Book 2169.   1964.   Reprint 1968.

The Illustrated Golden Bough.

Sir James George Frazer.

Macmillan London Ltd.   1978.

Editors. Mary Douglas & Sabine MacCormack.

BIBLIOGRAPHY

In the Wake of the Hurricane.

Bob Ogley.

Froglets Publications Ltd.   1987.

Chartwell, Kent. Guide Book.

The National Trust.   1992.   Reprint 1998.

Painting as a Pastime.

Winston Churchill His Life as a Painter.

Sotheby's Catalogue.   1998.

Speaking for Themselves.

The Personal Letters of Winston and Clementine Churchill.

Mary Soames.

Doubleday London.   1998.

In the Footsteps of Churchill.

Richard Holmes.

BBC Books Worldwide.   2005.

BIBLIOGRAPHY

Churchill & Chartwell.

The Untold Story of Churchill's Houses & Gardens.

Stefan Buczacki.

Frances Lincoln Ltd.   2007.

Unsolved East Anglian Murders.

Jonathon Sutherland & Diane Canwell.

Pen & Sword Books Ltd.   2007.

The Churchill Papers. Nov 1924 – Jul 1945.

CHAR 1/393A-C and CHAR 1/394

Churchill College Cambridge.

https://www.chu.cam.ac.uk

Westerham Heritage.

https://www.westerhamheritage.org.uk

Holy Trinity Church, Crockham Hill.

https://www.crockhamhillchurch.org/great-lives

EXTRACT FROM "BALDUR"

Retold by A & E Keary

So Frigga stood up, and called to her everything on earth that had power to hurt or slay. First she called all metals to her; and heavy iron-ore came lumbering up the hill into the crystal hall, brass and gold, copper, silver, lead, and steel, and stood before the Queen, who lifted her right hand high in the air, saying,

"Swear to me that you will not injure Baldur;"
and they all swore, and went.

Then she called to her all stones; and huge granite came with crumbling sandstone, and white lime, and the round smooth stones of the sea-shore, and Frigga raised her arm saying,

"Swear that you will not injure Baldur;"
and they swore, and went.

Then Frigga called to her the trees; and wide-spreading oak-trees, with tall ash and sombre firs came rushing up the hill with long branches, from which green leaves like flags were waving, and Frigga raised her hand and said,

"Swear that you will not hurt Baldur;"
and the said,

"We swear,"
and went.

207

After this, Frigga called to her the diseases who came blown thitherward by poisonous winds on wings of pain, and to the sound of moaning. Frigga said to them,

"Swear"

and they sighed,

"We swear,"

then flew away.

Then Frigga called to her all beasts, birds and venomous snakes, who came to her and swore, and disappeared. After this she stretched out her hand to Baldur, whilst a smile spread over her face, saying,

"And now, my son, you cannot die."

But just then Odin came in, and when he had heard from Frigga the whole story, he looked even more mournful than she had done; neither did the cloud pass from his face when he was told of the oaths that had been taken.

"Why do you still look so grave my Lord?" demanded Frigga, at last.

"Baldur cannot now die."

But Odin asked very gravely,

"Is the shadow gone out of our son's heart, or is it still there?"

"It cannot be there,"

said Frigga, turning away her head, and folding her hands before her.

But Odin looked at Baldur, and saw how it was. The hands pressed to the heavy heart, the beautiful brow grown dim. Then immediately he arose, saddled Sleipnir, his eight-footed steed, mounted him, and, turning to Frigga said,

"I know of a dead Vala, Frigga, who, when she was alive, could tell what was going to happen; her grave lies on the east side of Helheim, and I am going there to awake her, and ask whether any terrible grief, is really coming upon us."

*****